To Amos & Jackie

Enjoy !

Sol Reily

♡ Lee + Buck
March 4: 2022

JOHN WAYNE MIXSON

FLORIDA'S 39TH GOVERNOR

NARRATED BY:

GOVERNOR WAYNE MIXSON AND MARGIE GRACE MIXSON

WRITTEN BY:

SIDNEY W. RILEY

John Wayne Mixson: Florida's 39th Governor
Copyright © 2021 by Sidney W. Riley

ISBN: 978-1-949810-10-3

The Florida Historical Society Press
435 Brevard Avenue
Cocoa, FL 32922
http://myfloridahistory.org/fhspress

DEDICATION

This book is dedicated to Margie Grace Mixson and Judy Mathews Riley.

Two women of remarkable strengths . . .

ACKNOWLEDGMENTS

This book represents over three years of research, interviews, writing, and rewriting. The successful completion of this project could not have been realized without the assistance of many people. However, getting people who knew Wayne Mixson to help was always easy, since they all highly respected this great Florida legislator and wanted to help.

The most important contributing factor to this book was Margie Mixson's extensive library of photographs, newspaper clippings, and documents that covered everything from Wayne's early years through the legislative years, the campaign, and his time as Lieutenant Governor. This material, combined with many entertaining interviews with Wayne Mixson, along with some of his own writings, provided the core information in this book.

The eagerly provided help of Governor Bob Graham and his lovely wife, Adele, was another invaluable source of information. Bob Graham devoted significant time and attention to helping with the content and accuracy of the book. The fact that he and Adele contributed the final chapter to the book demonstrates their level of support.

Of course, the support and assistance of my beloved wife, Judy, was essential to completion of the project. Also, the support and participation of my wonderful daughter, Allison Rohlman, was another great contribution. This project was initiated because of the support of Bill Stanton, my dear friend, who has worked in industrial development in Jackson County for fifty years. Bill is also a good friend of Wayne Mixson, and he encouraged him to contact me for accomplishing the project.

Dale Cox, local author and historian, also provided assistance and support. His mother, Pearl, was also a friend of the Mixsons and provided encouragement. All of those who provided testimonials about their life experiences with Wayne Mixson created a valuable element of the work. These included Governor Bob Martinez and his wife, Mary Jane, Governor "Buddy" MacKay and his wife, Anne, Florida Senator Bill Nelson, Dr. Gregg Alexander, and Amos Morris. Since Wayne reached the fine old age of 98, he outlived most of his peers or this list of testimonials would have filled the book.

We hope that this book adds to the documentation of Florida's history during a period of great change in the state. A time of a new constitution, reorganization of government, tremendous growth and development, passage of vital, lasting legislation, and transition of political power.

FOREWORD

This book presents the life story of John Wayne Mixson, who served as a Florida state representative, Florida lieutenant governor, and briefly as the 39th governor of Florida. The results of his work while filling these important roles continues to positively impact the state of Florida and all of its citizens. It is hoped that this work will properly document the many contributions this great Florida statesman made to his state.

Wayne Mixson was a uniquely qualified man who performed in a unique capacity during a unique era of Florida's history. He was a child of the Great Depression, part of the "Greatest Generation," patriotically served his nation when he was called, became a top executive in Florida's agricultural industry, and then, as a legislator, served Florida when it most needed him.

The preparation for his future as a great legislator began as he was raised on a small South Alabama farm during the Depression years. These early experiences instilled many foundational personal values such as devotion to family, religious strengths, conservatism, respect for authority, work ethic, empathy for others, patriotism, pride, and a driving will to succeed.

His service in the military during World War II demonstrated his patriotism and belief in the principles that founded our nation. During these years his personal discipline was strengthened, his world view was enhanced, and he was offered the rare opportunity to enter a program that afforded him access to some of the finest colleges in the Northeast, as he advanced his education.

While gaining advanced learning as part of an officer preparation program, attending Columbia University, Denison University, and the Wharton School, he experienced life in the more liberal, industrialized, and diverse society of the Northeast. This wider perspective of different individual opinions would later become invaluable during his legislative career.

After the war ended, he completed his undergraduate degree in Business at the University of Florida. After graduating from the university, he immediately married his longtime sweetheart, Margie Grace of Graceville.

A personal, enduring devotion to farming and all aspects of agriculture was created by his boyhood experience on the family farm. Later, his experiences as a significant farmer in Jackson County, Florida, his years of work as a top executive and ambassador of the Florida Farm Bureau organization, and his many years of serving as a member and chairman of the Florida Agricultural Committee as a legislator, all combined to make him a lifetime advocate for agriculture.

As a beginning first-term legislator, Wayne Mixson's initial assignment was perhaps the most important of his career. He eagerly participated in the first reorganization of Florida's state government, and the first rewriting of the state Constitution, since 1885. This work resulted in a significant streamlining of state government by reducing suffocating "layering," removing obsolete agencies and requirements, strengthening the role of the executive branch, reorganizing the governor's cabinet by creating five appointed cabinet positions, enhancing the Department of Commerce, creating the concept of home rule for counties, establishing term limits for the governor, and creating a "declaration of rights" which defined citizens' rights, placed a ten-mill limit on local taxes, and made many other significant improvements. Most of these endure and serve today.

Shortly after the work on the constitution during his first term they passed Florida's famous Sunshine Law, which makes all government correspondence and records available to the public. It also restricted the activities of meetings among elected officials in order to reduce behind the scenes collusion and special deals.

Mixson initially served on the powerful Agricultural Committee, and during his second term became chairman, a position he held until he left the House of Representatives to become lieutenant governor. His work as an advocate of agriculture in Florida was of tremendous benefit to that sector of Florida's economy, and continues to serve farming interests. Among the legislative accomplishments during this era were (1) creation of the Green Belt Laws which protected farmers from excessive taxation as properties around them were developed, by taxing land based on its use, (2) creation of Florida's homestead exemption to provide fair taxation for residential property owners, (3) enactment of new legislation which provided a reasonable balance on use of pesticides in farming, reaching a balance between ecological and economic considerations.

During this era of Florida's political history, a profound transition was underway; and Representative Wayne Mixson played an instrumental role in enabling this change to occur without disruption, bitter conflict, or stalemate. The rural, conservative Democrats of North Florida had been the majority in the state legislature since Florida was created. However, in the post-World War II period retirees from the northern states began to migrate to new developments in South Florida. Finally, their numbers swelled to a point where they became the majority of Florida's citizens. A reapportionment, which was ordered in 1968, transferred political control from conservative North Florida politicians to the more liberal South Florida politicians. Wayne Mixson was to play a vital role in peacefully accomplishing this potentially volatile transition.

The insights that Wayne had acquired while living and attending schools in the Northeast, combined with his childhood conservative, rural foundations, enabled him to become an informal mediator between the new opposing political groups in Florida's legislature. He solidified this dual relationship when he assisted the South Florida group in getting an urban housing bill passed. He then became an instrument of compromise, assisting both sides in moving much legislation through passage. This rare, unofficial distinction made him an ideal running mate for the liberal South Florida politician, Senator Bob Graham, in his quest for the governorship.

With Wayne Mixson's influence on the North Florida voting, combined with Bob Graham's popularity in South Florida, their combined ticket readily won the election.

During their two terms in the executive branch, they accomplished an agenda of economic development, tourism enhancement, and environmental protections that moved Florida to the forefront. Much of their legislation and practices remain in effect decades later.

Most people of that era feel that Wayne Mixson could have easily become the next elected governor of Florida, but he decided to retire to his farm in Jackson County. He and his wife, Margie, have enjoyed many years of retirement, traveling, engaging in civic activities, and farming. Until Wayne's death in 2020, they resided in Tallahassee, Florida, still enjoying life and each other.

PART I

BUILDING THE FOUNDATION

1922–1967

Wayne Mixson entered politics at a relatively old age. His experiences during the forty-three years prior to running for the Florida legislature uniquely prepared him for the opportunity to serve the people of Florida for the next twenty years as a member of state government. It was the foundation that was laid during his earlier life that enabled him to become one of the leaders in state politics during his era of service.

Growing up and working on a small family farm in southern Alabama, being a child of the Great Depression, Wayne developed a strong Christian work ethic. Serving in the U.S. Navy during World War II, he developed an enduring spirit of patriotism. Attending recognized universities in the Northeast provided an excellent education and exposed him to problems related to urban living in the North. Graduating from the University of Florida (with honors) strengthened his ties to Florida. Becoming a major Jackson County landowner and member of the farming community built onto his lifelong love of the land and agriculture. Becoming a national executive for Farm Bureau, and lobbying on behalf of agricultural legislation in many states, taught him how state governments functioned and introduced him to many agricultural leaders and legislators.

With this experience behind him, Wayne Mixson was uniquely qualified to serve the people of Florida as he joined the Florida Legislature in 1967.

CHAPTER ONE

THE EARLY YEARS

Growing Up in Alabama

Wayne Mixson's life journey began on June 16, 1922, on a 160-acre, South Alabama farm owned by his parents, Cecil and Mineola Moseley Mixson. They named their firstborn son John Wayne Mixson, in recognition of the famed movie icon. From his birth, God graciously bestowed a great blessing by delivering Wayne into a conservative, loving, principled, Christian family with a long tradition of patriotism and service to our nation. The concepts of a productive life, assumption of responsibilities, Christian compassion for others, and strong work ethic that his parents were to demonstrate, teach, and ingrain within Wayne during his formative years would serve him well throughout his adult life.

At the time Wayne was born, over half of the families in the United States lived on farms. Eighty-five percent of these homes did not have electricity. Life on a farm required everyone in the family to work as a team. The Mixson family had a small dairy farm, and in those days, it was all hand milking.

Around the age of seven, Wayne actively began doing chores. The routine each day was to rise early, milk before school, attend school, and then milk again when he got home from school. And the cows had to be milked every day, including Saturday and

Sunday. His daily duties also included all feeding of the pigs, chickens, and mules. Water was provided using a hand pump for filling water troughs. Daily chores were a full-time, unending job on the farm.

Wayne recalls, "This demanding farm regimen helped ingrain a strong work ethic within all of the family. It was necessary and was the way everyone around you lived. Nothing was free. The government was not going to come along and give you what you needed to survive. It demanded self-reliance for yourself, your family, and your neighbors. It built strong families and strong communities. I think it prepared us for the hardships that were ahead.

"Our family farm was located on a dirt, rural road near the New Brockton, Alabama, community near the Florida border. The house was typical of rural farm homes across the nation during that era. It did not have electricity or indoor plumbing and had no running water. We were finally able to electrify our house in 1941, when the REA began. Most of our food came from the family garden, another unending job. My two sisters were still too young for these chores, so most of it fell on me.

"My Mother prepared nourishing meals on a wooden cook stove, and perishables were kept in a gas-powered refrigerator. The house was heated by two fireplaces, and lighting during the evenings was provided by gas lamps. The family enjoyed many evenings listening to the family radio, and we always had a delivered daily newspaper.

"These were our primary contacts with the outside world. Some evenings members of the family enjoyed playing music on a variety of instruments, including the violin, mandolin, guitar, and piano."

Wayne's oldest sister, Miriam, was born in 1927 when he was five years old. She also grew up on the farm, and when she was old enough to help, she assumed a portion of the chores that the farm demanded. After graduation from high school, she worked at a local bank for a few years. Then she married a local Jackson County, Florida, farmer, Durelle Johnson, and worked as a homemaker. Miriam and Durelle had two children, Carol and Stanley.

Along with his successful farming business, Durelle was an active participant in local politics. He served several successive terms as a Jackson County commissioner, representing the Graceville District.

In 1931 Wayne's second sister, Margaret, was born. After finishing high school she attended Troy University, and earned her certification to teach at the high school level. She married Cecil Costin Jr., a man from Port St. Joe. The Costin family was one of the old, prominent families in that community, working as merchants and in the booming coastal real estate development market. Cecil was a young lawyer, a graduate of the University of Florida Law School.

As a young girl, Margaret was always interested in outdoor activities. She always wanted to ride the most spirited horse and drive the biggest tractor. Margaret and Cecil had two children, Renee and Charles. After working in law for several years, Cecil served several terms in the Florida legislature. He also practiced law and developed coastal real estate in the region.

Margaret and Cecil both loved the outdoors. They were torn between the Florida coast and the North Carolina mountains, so they enjoyed both. They bought a home in the mountains and spent many summer months enjoying the cool weather and the fine golf courses in the area. At other times they enjoyed Florida with its ocean, beaches, fishing, tennis, horseback riding, and quail shooting.

The Mixson Family Ancestry

"I am proud of my family heritage. The men and women who preceded me in our lineage accomplished much and actively

5

participated in defending and building our nation. I cannot omit them from mention in the story of my life," Wayne asserts.

"My pioneer ancestors first arrived on these shores from England in 1650. John Mixon, later spelled Mixson, arrived from England as an indentured servant[1] on the ship *Guiding Star*, and settled near the Rappahannock River, in what is now Richmond County, Virginia. This is only twenty-five miles south of Mt. Vernon, George Washington's home. Several of the Mixson clan fought with Washington during the Revolutionary War.

"On May 22, 1650, Captain Moore Fauntleroy[2] was deeded 5,350 acres of land on the north side of the Rappahannock River in the English colony of Virginia. Each of the 107 headrights received fifty acres after working four to five years for the landlord. Today the community of Farnham, Virginia, in Richmond County marks this site on Highway 3, which is called "History Highway." Fauntleroy descendants still reside on what was the original plantation. Also, in nearby Jamestown, the telephone directory contains numerous Mixons. In the ensuing years, the Mixson family moved south to North Carolina, then on to Georgia. The families of both of my grandparents finally arrived in what is today Coffee County, Alabama, in 1850. It was new territory at that time.

"As citizens of the state of Alabama, the Mixson family continued to answer the call to duty when they were needed. My great-grandfather and two great-uncles all served in the Alabama legislature. In fact, it was my great-grandfather who, in the 1850s introduced and passed a bill which approved negotiations with officials from the state of Florida for the annexation of West Florida into Alabama. Although the concept appealed to the Alabama officials, it did not strike a positive chord with the officials in Florida. These negotiations ended with the onset of the Civil War. The Mixsons of Alabama again rose to serve during the Civil War, with several family members participating in the Confederate army. My great-grandfather and two uncles served, and we heard many stories describing their campaigns, service, and hardships.

There were several veterans of World War I who lived in our neighborhood. They had fought in the trenches in France and had been involved in terrible battles in Argonne, Somme, Verdun, and other sites near what are now Belgium, France, and Netherlands. I remember sitting enthralled as they described the horrors of these events. Sometimes they gave me rifle shells and other items from the war. These stories especially frightened me because in the late 1930s war talk was increasing because of Hitler's aggressive actions in Europe."

Growing Up on the Farm—Childhood Years

Those were comfortable years for Wayne as a child growing up on the farm. Wayne's parents were debt-free and had title to their farm and home. This was to become very important in the Depression era that was looming ahead. The future looked promising for farmers in the 1920s. Indeed, progress was being made both technologically and financially for most farmers. While he was a youth, his father bought another 160-acre farm located about two miles away from their home, thus doubling his farm operation. Mr. Mixson was an intelligent, hard worker and good manager. His extended family included farmers, merchants, and sawmillers.

"I remember how proud my father was when he bought a new automobile, a 'Dixie Flyer.' The car was manufactured in Louisville, Kentucky, from 1916 through 1923. The company ceased operations during the post-World War I recession. Today it would be quite valuable as a vintage automobile. He also bought the first rubber-tired tractor in Coffee County in 1939. It was a huge step forward in farming, going into mechanized tractor farming instead of using mule teams.

"It was sad to see the mule begin to become obsolete. There was something special about working with a good mule team. Each had its own personality, usually involving stubbornness and arrogance. We had four mules, whose names were Gray, Bill, Scrap, and Peanut. Old Bill was gentle, slow, and tended to take orders well, so Dad usually gave him to me for plowing. We also had some horses for working with the cattle. Horses were not good for plowing because they tended to be nervous and walked too fast," Wayne recalls.

"There was a story about an agricultural adviser who came down to Alabama from Washington. He reportedly said that the Alabama farmers were stupid because they always had to buy mules instead of getting a male and a female and raising their own mules. Of course, the mule is a hybrid cross between a horse and a donkey and cannot reproduce."

Comforted by the booming economy of the mid- and late 1920s, the family built a new house across the road and painted it a gleaming white. The house stood out from most of the surrounding structures in the surrounding farm community where homes and farm buildings were generally made from virgin longleaf pine timber. Since this wood would never rot, structures were seldom adorned with paint.

Wayne says he can clearly remember the day they moved into their new, gleaming, spacious home. "I recall carrying a small chair from our old house over to our new residence. At this time we had a telephone, but electricity did not come until 1941, my senior year in high school. I assisted the electrician while he wired our house for electricity.

"In the kitchen we had a kerosene-burning gas refrigerator. This was also considered a modern marvel at the time, since most homes used insulated ice boxes and had ice delivered from the local ice distributor.

"During the winter, while the leaves were off the trees, from our farm you could see across the valley to another farm which was about a mile away. This was the Folsom farm, where Governor Jim Folsom[3] was raised. I find it remarkable that two governors, one serving in Alabama and the other (me), serving in Florida, were raised in rural Alabama on adjoining farms."

Church

When asked about his early relationships with religion, Wayne replied, "During my life I have been involved with three church denominations, Baptist, Methodist, and Pentecostal. My parents loved to entertain the church family,·and after church on many Sundays we would have guests for a meal and singing. My Father was active in the church, usually keeping the books and financial records. We were always in the church, even going to singing schools during the summer . . . although it didn't help me much.

"There were two churches located less than half a mile from our house, a Baptist and a Methodist. Neither could afford a full-time preacher, so they both held services every other Sunday, on an alternating schedule. We attended Sunday school and services every Sunday, going to where the service was held. The congregations at these rural churches were small, and they had little revenue for church needs. The Methodist Church finally had to sell the church building to the Pentecostal Church. This congregation was quite a bit larger, and our family continued to alternate between the two local churches. The Pentecostal singing and services were much more spirited and lively, and we found it to be our favorite. Many new faces came to this church from the Bible college in New Brockton. My Father would occasionally host hunting and fishing outings for these student preachers. Often on Sunday afternoons we gathered around the piano and sang those spirited gospel songs. I continue to love many of those songs. For me, it was a great period and a great venue for growing up. Safe, secure, and enjoying hours of play romping in the yard around the house, and in the barnyard around the barn. Life was good!"

1929 and Depression Times

Then, suddenly, things changed. With a loud crash which shook the world, the stock market began a disastrous plunge on October 29, 1929, which is remembered as "Black Tuesday." This was the onset of the Great Depression which led to almost half of the nation's banks failing, thousands of homes' savings becoming worthless, farms being foreclosed, approximately forty percent of the stock market's value being lost, and unemployment rising to almost thirty percent.

For the next decade, misery and struggle dominated the economy and most American families. The economic collapse started in 1929 and steadily became worse through the mid-1930s. About 1937 the situation began to improve slightly as a result of the government programs which had been started to improve employment and get some money circulating. Then there was a relapse and the situation returned to an economic low. It was not until the war in Europe during the end of the decade that things began to recover. It was a long, devastating depression. Wayne's generation was challenged with surviving the Great Depression and then World War II. "I am proud of the way Americans rose to these challenges and succeeded. I am proud to be part of the Greatest Generation," Wayne states proudly.

Agriculture was among those sectors most severely impacted during the Great Depression. After the historic crash of the stock market, prices for farm products declined rapidly and by the spring of 1933, the agricultural sector was approaching disaster status. Nationally, twenty-five percent of farm workers, and an even higher percentage of all non-farm workers, were jobless.

There was no welfare. Many families had little to eat, many others lost their farms and homes. Homeless individuals roamed the country, and often hopped rides aboard freight trains that were crisscrossing the nation. Many lived day-to-day, seeking day labor and odd jobs for income or food. A major part of the clothing worn by many people was handmade from flour and fertilizer sacks. Other clothing in their wardrobes had patches sewn on top of patches. Minor children were often forced to work and help the family survive instead of attending school. The going rate for work was fifty cents per day. The work was usually hoeing and chopping crops in the growing season, and picking cotton in the fall.

"I vividly remember on several occasions when my father had me go to the corn crib to shuck and shell some of our corn for a needy family that was at the door. We were fortunate, since we could grow much of the food we needed. Families would show up at our door, desperate and begging for food . . . literally starving. We could not refuse them. We would also take some of our corn and grind it to make bread. My parents would prepare a bag containing bread, some potatoes, beans, syrup, and other food we grew on the farm. I am proud of my parents for their giving spirit.

"The situation was especially difficult for widows with children, and there were many of them. My aunt had six children when her husband died in his mid-thirties. She had nowhere to go. Father built her a small house from rough lumber salvaged from an old building on the farm. Her children, my first cousins, worked in the fields and picked cotton with me. Finally, the older ones left for jobs as they came of age. Some of them joined the Civilian Construction Corps (CCC)[4] and worked on public projects. They were paid $28 per month, but at least they were working and surviving. They always sent part of their pay to their mother to help her. That was the way many families made it through those terrible years. People appreciated the kind words of President Franklin Roosevelt and his attempts to help, but it seemed many of the programs didn't make sense.

"Across the land many struggling families lived on dried beans, potatoes, canning from the farms, milk, and eggs. Some would swap eggs for sugar and salt with the 'Rolling Store'[5] which would travel to us once per week. Meat was all raised on the farms and was shared among those living and working on the farm. Everyone had a big vegetable garden where they grew vegetables and sweet and Irish potatoes.

"We were very fortunate. My family owned and operated a four-mule farm. Dad's family owned and operated a country store. Since we were farmers we could grow most of the food we needed; we had chickens and cows and made our own syrup. Our family unit helped each other. Importantly, we had almost no debts.

Times were rough for all farmers, but it was even worse for many others. It was especially bad for the people who were in debt or those who were unemployed. Cotton prices fell as low as five cents per pound, with a 500-pound bale bringing $25. Acreage yield was around ½ bale per acre, or $12.50 per acre. This meant that a 100-acre farm would yield only $1,250 per year from its main crop. Many farms operated at a loss and were forced to tum to a bank for a farm loan, using their land as collateral. Many farm loans were issued through the Federal Land Bank, since few local banks were willing to engage in farm financing. Also, property taxes had to be paid. I remember occasions when farmers had to sell some of their mules to raise money for taxes on the family farm.

"Farmers who had been successful operators found themselves unable to pay back their loans. Foreclosed farms flooded the market, depressing land values to a few dollars per acre. Much of this land was bought by large corporations and timber operations. After the war ended many of these speculators made fortunes when they sold these lands.

"The government began many public works projects in order to create jobs. In 1929 the city of Elba had experienced a disastrous flood. As a public project, the government decided to help the city by building a levee along the river to prevent future floods. As an investment to help our needs, my father bought a dump truck which was used on this project.

"At that time there was not a single paved road in Coffee County outside of a city limit. The county was filled with rough, unpaved rural roads winding through clay hills. When it rained many of these roads became impassable. Federal public project funding for helping pave these roads was generous during the Depression. Father bought more trucks and participated in building and paving many of these roads. He was very busy running the farm and managing these trucks, but it greatly helped our family through those difficult years."

The federal government attempted to help the farmers, but it was difficult to ascertain if they were aiding or only adding to the misery. Some notable farm measures introduced during the Depression were:

1. Agricultural Adjustment Act (AAA) gave economic aid to farmers.
2. Commodity Credit Corporation purchased goods to be stored until prices were higher.
3. Soil Conservation Service was another government agency providing relief to farmers. They also promoted practices that protected land from erosion. Funding was provided for some erosion programs.

Some government programs helped farmers live through the 1930s, but this change affected the future of agriculture forever. Government became a major component of farming. By 1940 nearly six million farmers were receiving federal subsidies.

Wayne continues, "I was seven years old when the market crashed and the Depression began. I would be seventeen when it ended with the onset of World War II. The lessons learned during that era of struggle and sacrifice impacted my family and impacted me, forever etching us with conservative principles and outlook.

"I remember that my father, along with most other farmers we knew, resented government interference in our farming operations. As part of their failed attempts to manipulate and support farm product prices under the Agricultural Adjustment Act, they implemented quotas to reduce the farm output, in order to reduce supply and raise prices. They did this while the public was standing in bread lines without enough food, and farms were being foreclosed. It caused us to lose a lot of respect for the federal government and its farm programs.

"They sent inspectors to the farms to be sure output was within the quota limits they had arbitrarily set for the farm. I recall when they had my father plow up several acres of cotton and told him he would have to kill several piglets because of the quotas . . . and they could not be consumed for food. All a farmer could do was obey their demands, and initially there was no payment made to the farm for the losses they caused.

"The farmer could not see any benefit from killing his pigs or plowing up his cotton when he needed every penny that he could get to cover the cost of his operations. He and his family were struggling for survival, and this government agent was making him destroy things of value. Later, some of their programs accomplished some gains for farmers, but nothing really worked until we entered World War II.

A familiar jingle from the Depression era, which my father used to quote, clearly shows the resentful emotions evoked by these socialistic programs. I can still recite it from memory. It goes like this:

"LITTLE BOY BLUE"

Little Boy Blue come blow your horn,
There is a Government Agent counting your corn,
Another is lecturing the old red sow
On how many pigs she can have, and how.

Pa's gone to town to find out what
He can do next month with the old meadow lot,
Ma's at the radio hearing them tell,
How under the "New Deal" there ain't no Hell.

Aunt Mamie is in Washington drawing big pay,
From the PDQ and the AAA,
The hired man quit when his work didn't please,
And got himself a job trimming government trees.

They will be telling you soon if you don't take care,
Where you can live and what you can wear,
What you can pay for your pants and your shoes,
So this is no time to be taking a snooze.

Little Boy Blue may be buried deep,
Under the red tape ... but he is not asleep!"

At ninety-eight, Wayne enjoys astounding friends when he quotes that Depression-era poem.

Growing Up on the Farm—Teen Years

Growing up on the Mixson farm was not only a great place to play and experience nature, it was also a learning experience. There were always chores to be done which were assigned to Wayne and were his sole responsibilities. It was part of developing a good work ethic and handling responsibilities.

Wayne continues, "Although the work was always given first priority, I did find enough freedom to enjoy time with my cousins for hunting, fishing, swimming in local farm ponds, hiking, playing baseball, biking, and riding horses. Many of our toys were hand-built, using farm tools. I have great memories of roaming and exploring the fields and climbing favorite trees. I recall several occasions when we swam and dove in nearby streams, searching for Indian relics. I still have and treasure some of the relics we found on those expeditions.

"My parents always gave me a few cows to care for and call my own. By the time I came home from serving in the Navy, these had grown into a small herd of over twenty cows. Later these would become my own 'seed stock' and would grow into a herd of hundreds."

Remembering the "Goat Story"

This is one of Wayne's favorite childhood stories. "Once, my uncle Roscoe gave me two goats, 'Billy' and 'Nanny.' As is the law of nature, the first thing on the mind of Billy was to begin raising a family. Since the breeding cycle for a female goat is very frequent, the goat family tends to increase in size very rapidly. This growth can create problems. Since the grass always seems to be greener on the other side of the fence, the goats tended to want to eat through a fence, which is not a good idea if your head is sporting a set of horns. This situation would often require me to go around the perimeter of the pasture after school to liberate half of the herd from the fence.

"The goats despised getting wet in the rain. During storms, many of the stronger goats would jump the fence and find refuge in any convenient shelter, including our covered front porch. During some rainstorms it appeared as if the entire herd of over fifty goats was huddled on our porch. Of course, after their huddle on the front porch it had to be cleaned. I was the designated scrubber since I owned the goats.

"The herd developed two powerful enemies when their numbers approached fifty. My mother was intent to keep them off the porch, and my Dad was intent to keep them from grazing in the cow pastures. As a result of these ongoing problems, after an extended rainy period it was decided that it was time for the goats to go! Mother was determined to rid her front porch of goats.

"It was an emotional moment for me to part with the goats when I discovered that I could only get $.50 per head, barely enough for me to buy myself a bicycle. I was not sure my goat enterprise had really been successful. Goat farming can be a tough business."

The Politics of the Time

Wayne explains the political attitudes during these difficult times. "There was a significant difference in the political attitudes of my mother's family, the Moseleys, and my father's family, the Mixsons. Most people of the day were fairly well-informed. My father's family had some serious reservations about whether or not it had been advisable for Alabama to secede during the Civil War. They tended to be conservative Republicans. Mother's family were ardent 'Yellow Dog' Democrats. That is a term used to describe a Democrat who always votes a straight party ticket under any circumstances. Thus, there was tension between the two families whenever politics were discussed. The Civil War had only ended seventy-five or eighty years previously, and was still a 'hot' topic of discussion."

School Days

Wayne attended elementary school at the Mixson Cross Road School, which was one of the many small, two-room, two-teacher schools serving students across Coffee County, Alabama, and most other rural counties across the South. His schoolmates were all from other small farms in the local cotton farming area. Students walked to school for distances up to two miles since there were no school buses and few families had automobiles. Those who lived closest to the school usually walked home for lunch. Students who lived further away brought their lunch.

At the Mixson Cross Road School, a lone teacher taught in the "Little Room," which covered the first four grades. It was always an important step in a student's development when he graduated from the Little Room to the "Big Room," where he would remain until he finished the eighth grade. The total school enrollment was forty to fifty students. Many of Wayne's classmates had to work part-time on the farm and had to drop out of school before they finished the eighth grade in order to help their family survive.

Wayne describes what a school day was like. "The school day at my elementary school began with chapel, and all students assembled in one of the rooms. This assembly always included Bible reading, reciting the Lord's prayer, and singing, which we did with great gusto, especially when we sang rounds. This was when we sang a song where we were divided into three groups, with each group singing a different part.

"Every Friday afternoon a spelling bee was held in the Big Room. Everyone competed in this great learning experience. I found it to be an advantage to be in a single room with students working in grades ahead of my current grade. I would always listen intently while the teacher was working with those advanced grades, and I found that what I heard and learned often helped me excel in my own grade. This was especially true for me in math.

"Every day we would be assigned homework. Each morning the teacher would bring in our graded homework papers and review the problems and answers class by class. By listening to the reviews for the two or three levels ahead of me, I remained far ahead of my class level.

"Our books were not furnished by the school system. Each of us had to buy our own books. Thus, there was a great demand for used books, so we all took great care of our books in order to assure they would get a high price when we sold them at the end of the term.

"After working through all class levels on one subject, the teacher would then move to the next subject and begin working with each class level again in succession. My listening technique worked for all subjects. I always loved sports and played basketball, touch football, and baseball during these years.

"The school term for most county schools covered seven months, while city schools lasted nine months. One year the Depression was so severe that the county schools had to close about mid-term. This caused all of the students to repeat their grade the following year unless they could pass a course test which was given county-wide. I remember taking the test that was required for me to pass from the seventh grade into the eighth grade. I made it.

"The next year all of the county schools were consolidated into five towns in the county. I entered the eighth grade attending the consolidated school in Elba, which was considered one of the best. One day my eighth-grade math teacher, Mrs. Ham, asked me to stand up in front of the entire class of thirty-five students. Then she announced that I was one of only two students countywide with a perfect score on the math test. I felt I was ready to compete with these city kids.

"I attended Elba High School through my tenth grade. By this time there were school buses running in the county, and the daily ride from Mixson Cross Roads to Elba was a fifteen-mile trip on sloppy clay roads through hilly, country areas. On numerous occasions we would be late for school because the bus had slipped off the road into the ditch, and we lost time waiting to be pulled out of a ditch by a mule team from a nearby farm. Some days we never made it to school. Although there were some disadvantages, I did benefit greatly from attending school in Elba. The teachers were great, and I enjoyed many of the school sports and other activities. I even joined the literary society.

"My eleventh grade offered new opportunities. The school bus to Elba was still available, but a new bus route from our farm to New Brockton schools had been started, and the ride was only eight miles. Students in grades eleven and twelve were allowed to drive school buses in the county, and the principal at the New Brockton High School asked me if I would drive this new route. I became a paid bus driver in the eleventh grade.

"The route for this bus included a circular route to and from Mixson Cross Roads and another circular route of eight miles in a different area. The school system paid me $10 per month to drive these two routes each day, which I did for my last two years in high school.

"Bus driving was a very interesting learning experience for me. I never had any trouble in any way, except one morning after giving some riders repeated warnings that the bus couldn't sit and wait for them every morning, I finally took action. I left three kids from one family after a reasonable wait for them to come out of their house. My principal, Mr. Roberson, the man I adored more than any other man on earth (except for my father), said to me, 'Mixson, you wouldn't intentionally leave any kids behind would you?'

"In time, I became the driver that Mr. Roberson would come to when he had a special task, such as taking a sick student home in his personal car. Another task of taking his car to the post office to pick up the school mail every day was assigned to me. I was 'on call' daily for every task that came up which required a driver.

The responsibilities and trust he placed upon me were important aspects of my development.

"At school I was an active student, involved in many school activities including plays, events, clubs, and sports. I was on the basketball team, which was highly regarded at that time. Our coach used a two-platoon system, which involved every player on the squad. My specialty was a long shot from the outside, which would be a three-pointer by today's rules. On the baseball team I pitched and played third base. Since I also had to drive the bus every day after school, it was impossible for me to attend all of the practice sessions, but I still made the starting team.

"I had to leave our house very early each morning in order to start the bus routes. Then during the evening I would get home late after making those same routes after school. This made keeping up with my farm chores more difficult, but that was just part of farm life. I was a busy young boy. However, I consider all of my high school years as a very happy, productive period of my life-journey.

"Although I had a lot of responsibilities and did hard work to accomplish them, times were even rougher for many of my classmates. It was just the way life was, and we had to do what was required. I graduated from New Brockton High School in 1941. None of us would ever have imagined that before the end of the year our nation would be immersed in a horrible world war, and that history would designate us as part of 'The Greatest Generation.'[6] Our destiny lay before us."

Endnotes

1. Indentured servitude was a labor system where people paid for their passage to the New World by working for an employer for a certain number of years. It was widely employed in the 18th century in the British colonies in North America and elsewhere. It was especially used as a way for the poor in Britain and the German states to obtain passage to the American colonies.

2. Capt. Moore Fauntleroy, the captain of the ship on which the Mixon family traveled, received 450 acres of land on the Rappahannock River on the north side of Swan Bay on May 22, 1650, for transporting 9 individuals including, George Underwood, his wife Mary and Anne Underwood. He relinquished the rights to this land to make good the patent on the other side of the river for 5350 acres of land. This info can be verified in Patent Book 2, p. 195. (C-2394) On this same day he received 1800 acres on the north side of the river adjoining the land of William Underwood for transporting 36 persons.

3. James Elisha Folsom Sr. (October 9, 1908-November 21, 1987), commonly known as Jim Folsom or Big Jim Folsom, was the 42nd governor of Alabama, having served from 1947 to 1951, and again from 1955 to 1959. Born in Coffee County in southeastern Alabama, Folsom was among the first southern governors to embrace integration and enforcement of civil rights for black Americans.

4. The Civilian Construction Corps (CCC) was one of the major federal programs initiated during the Great Depression in order to put men back to work The Civilian Conservation Corps was a public work relief program that operated from 1933 to 1942 in the United States for unemployed, unmarried men from relief families as part of the New Deal. The program provided jobs related to development of natural resources in rural lands owned by federal, state, and local government.

5. In the past, rural areas in the South were populated with families on small subsistence farms, sharecroppers, and field laborers. During these times, rolling store merchants were fairly abundant throughout Alabama, plying their trade on dusty dirt roads winding through the countryside. In Pike County alone, it is estimated that there were at least 25 rolling stores operating before World War II. While most people still made periodic trips to town for supplies, the rolling store was an added convenience to them and a necessity for those who were not able to get into town to shop. The stores serviced

regular routes so that customers could expect the truck to roll up and toot its horn the same time each week.

6. This term was first coined by Thomas John "Tom" Brokaw, an American television journalist and author best known as the anchor and managing editor of NBC Nightly News from 1982 to 2004. He is the author of *The Greatest Generation*, which was published in 1998, and other books. He is also the recipient of numerous awards and honors. He is the only person to host all three major NBC News programs.

CHAPTER TWO

WORLD WAR II

1941–A Year with "A Day to Be Remembered in Infamy"

Wayne Mixson was an eighteen-year-old teenager who had just earned his high school diploma and war drums were beating loudly across Europe as Germany's Adolf Hitler invaded and conquered nation after nation. England had entered the war against Germany and was under vicious aerial attack, as their army fought in Europe. Although America had not yet entered the conflict, America's industries were running at full capacity, sending needed supplies to England. If the United States chose to enter the war, Wayne Mixson was a prime candidate for enlistment.

Wayne vividly remembers this phase of his life. "I graduated from New Brockton High School in the spring of 1941. War had begun in Europe, but a strong isolationist sentiment across the nation was restricting the involvement of the United States in the conflict. However, we were switching much of our industrial capacity into military items in support of England and our European allies.

"The day after I graduated, I hitchhiked to Panama City, Florida, and became employed by the construction project which was at that time busy building Tyndall Field, near Panama City. That exposure sparked an interest in aviation within me. I realized that I needed to increase my level of technical training if I wanted to move ahead in my career. After researching my opportunities, I enrolled in Anderson Aircraft School in Nashville, Tennessee. I was planning to become an aircraft mechanic, aviation metalsmith, and general mechanic. After completing this training in 1942, I went back to work at Tyndall Air Force Base, this time as an aviation mechanic, maintaining the aircraft which were stationed there. It was during this period that I first met Margie.

"The year of 1941 was a remarkably difficult time to be suddenly thrust out of the high school environment and required to forge out a meaningful career. The world was in a precarious situation. Hitler's aggression in Europe was enveloping England and the European continent into war. Meanwhile, the population of the United States and most of the rest of the world was still struggling for basic essentials in the throes of the Great Depression. The emerging war economy was beginning to put people back to work, but times were still tough.

"It appeared to me that opportunities were scarce for having a successful career in agriculture. Frequently new graduates had no option except to remain on their small family farms as laborers, just to help their families survive. Many young boys and girls in the local Pea River Valley[1] region, and all across rural America, were like me. We were looking and listening in an attempt to determine what to do with their lives. Even though the economy had improved slightly, the nation was still in the grip of the Great Depression. It was a tough time to be entering the job market.

"At that time most families did not have a history or culture of advanced education. They had grown up in the midst of an era where economic opportunities were scarce. A large percentage of adults had not completed high school. Most farm children of that period realized that after they finished their education, they would have to leave the farm.

"After the vicious Japanese attack on Pearl Harbor on that Day of Infamy, many of my generation rushed to enlist in the conflict as a strong wave of nationalism swept across the land. Some waited for a call from the draft board, but most of the able-bodied young men answered the call. Some claimed they joined in order to have a place to sleep and to get something to eat. I was in Birmingham, Alabama, visiting a cousin when the announcement about the attack was made. We were watching a Lana Turner movie when they stopped the film and a man stepped onto the stage and told the audience what had transpired. It created quite a bit of excitement. The next day the two of us went to the recruiting office and attempted to enlist. However, after some consideration and discussion with my father, I decided to wait a few months.

"I found it amazing to see the women of our nation rise to meet the common challenge. As men left their jobs to enter military service, their positions were quickly filled by women. It became common to see women wearing hard hats and doing construction jobs that had always been considered man's work."

Answering the "Call to Arms"

"In October of 1942, at the age of nineteen, I voluntarily enlisted in the U.S. Navy. I was sent to the famous boot camp for the Navy at Great Lakes Naval Training Station, Great Lakes, Illinois. Upon arrival, we were all given a general classification test, which became a determining factor on what direction your navy career was going to take. When I took that test, I never realized how important the results would be in my future years.

"The first two months of boot camp involved the traditional disciplined training, drilling, and planned harassment to build our character. I recall once when one of our guys threw an envelope into the trash can one night after lights out. When the petty officer came by on inspection and found it, he sounded the gong and called everybody out. We had to carry that can four miles to the dump, discard the envelope, and then carry the can back four miles to the barracks. That kind of disciplined training was probably needed by a lot of those guys, but my training back on the farm had already prepared me. I knew what the mandates were and, although I might not like it, I was going to do what was expected.

"On one occasion while at Norman, Oklahoma, I had a two-week gap between classes, so they put me on KP (Kitchen Patrol) duty. I was placed in charge of the butter. While the serving line was passing by, I would take a specially designed fork and expertly place a cube of butter on top of your potatoes. I enjoyed that work, since it gave me a chance to talk momentarily with everyone there. I ended up making a deal with the pastry cook that I would furnish the butter if he would furnish the cookies, and it was a pretty good deal for us both.

"Finally we were moved into what was called the OGU, or the outgoing unit. After a ten-day leave for Christmas we were shipped out, most of the class going to assignments somewhere in the fleet. I was among a group that had been selected for additional training. I received orders to report to Naval Air Technical Training Center, Norman, Oklahoma, near the campus of the University of Oklahoma. At this training center I was entered into a six-month course in Navy aviation, including metalwork and general aircraft maintenance. I finished this course in June and was expecting to be shipped out to some active naval service station."

Becoming a Navy Airman

"Our duty assignments were posted on a designated barracks bulletin board. There were 253 seamen in the class, and the top five graduates were assigned to 'lighter than air,' the Navy blimps.[2] I was fortunate to be in the top five in class ranking.

"The rest of the class went to New Caledonia in the South Pacific. This was at the time of the Battle of the Coral Sea, when we were attempting to rout the Japanese out of Guadalcanal and halt their expansion into New Guinea. If allowed to continue their advance, they would reach Australia and New Zealand.

"I was given the choice of being assigned to Sunnyvale, California, or Lakehurst, New Jersey. I chose Lakehurst, which was the mother station for the lighter than air Navy blimp program. I was very aware of the story and disastrous fate of the German dirigible, the Hindenburg, which had been destroyed while landing at Lakehurst. However, I knew very little about the role of the non-rigid aircraft at that time. I was somewhat relieved when I discovered that our blimps were using the inert gas, helium, instead of the explosive gas, hydrogen, which was used by the Germans. Also, I knew that America had the U.S. *Dayton*, and there were many of those huge, rigid ships that were performing admirably.

"These aircraft were a tribute to Germany's superior engineering, so I considered being assigned to this elite group of airmen a great opportunity. I went from Oklahoma to Lakehurst for training. When I first saw our Navy blimp I was overwhelmed by its large size. Although it was not as big as the Hindenburg, it was much larger than I had imagined.

"We used an L-Ship for training, which was about the size of today's Goodyear blimp. It contained around 125,000 cubic feet of helium. The K-Ship, which we would later fly on active patrol, was significantly larger, holding 416,000 cubic feet of helium. It was about 250 feet long, almost the length of a football field. The gondola where the crew was contained was 45 feet long, about the size of a city bus.

"The normal crew was ten to twelve men, but usually we carried additional crew because of the long patrol periods. We had two 550-horsepower engines, burned about thirty gallons of gasoline per hour, and could cruise at eighty miles per hour in still conditions. Of course, it seemed the wind was always blowing against us.

"You can have some exciting landings when the wind is blowing and you are in a 'light' condition, as we usually were when coming home after a long trip. The earliest missions for these airships were escort and patrol. Early in 1942 we were suffering heavy marine losses losing ships and materials from German U-boat submarine attacks. We had not yet begun to organize cross-Atlantic convoys, even though we were shipping massive tonnage containing ships, vehicles, food, munitions, and aircraft to England and Russia. We tried at that time to ship some 5,000 tanks to Russia and only about half of them reached their destination across the North Sea.

"Admiral King, who was the Chief of Naval Operations,[3] was primarily concerned about naval operations in the Pacific, and had not yet begun to provide the east coast convoys with military escorts. He felt that evasive, zig-zag courses would enable ships to run the Atlantic. Unfortunately, the German submarines were waiting just a few miles off the eastern coast of the United States, and they were enjoying tremendous success.

"Debris was washing up on our beaches from Miami to Boston. Several of our ships were sunk within sight of Miami Beach. Many ships were intercepted, attacked, and sunk after only a few miles into their journey. These slow freighters were sitting ducks for the German submarines who usually attacked in 'wolf packs.'

"As the volume of movement of equipment and supplies increased, and these German attacks increased, the Navy began to organize convoys of ships. These convoys would make the Atlantic crossing in a large group of ships which were escorted by navy blimps, destroyers, and naval escort carriers.

"The blimps could provide escort during the most dangerous portion of the trip, which was the first 300 miles of the route. The blimps could hover above the convoy, moving at a slow speed. These airships were armed with 500-pound bombs and machine guns.

"The enemy submarines had to come up to near the surface in order to use their periscopes and to fire torpedoes. This made them visible to the escort blimps and subject to attack from above. Our blimp crews were very proud of the fact that, throughout the war, not a single ship was lost while under blimp escort. Blimps were a very effective defense force within their range of coverage.

"Land-based, fixed-wing aircraft, planes flying from the naval escort carriers, and the naval escort destroyers provided protection for the convoy during the mid-ocean portion of the trip. Within a few months after this convoy escort system was implemented, the losses from submarine attacks were vastly diminished.

"Although our blimps were not capable of rescuing people from the water, we were invaluable for search and rescue. We could move over the search area at a relatively slow speed and close to the surface, making detection of those in need much easier. When a blimp found survivors in the water, they would radio the position to nearby rescue-equipped equipment. We did carry survival gear, medical supplies, food, water, and large rafts which we often dropped down to them as we hovered 150 to 200 feet above them. We could even yell instructions and reassurance down to them.

"The convoys would assemble and depart from ports along the eastern seaboard, such as Philadelphia, Charleston, Norfolk, and others. We would stay with them for around 300 miles out to sea, flying back and forth over the convoy of hundreds of ships which were strung out for lengths up to twenty miles. We had several types of submarine detection devices, including devices which detected variances in the earth's magnetic field which could be caused by objects under us in the water. Also, we had radar and sonar detection systems. We carried buoys that we could drop and then read beams in the water. Usually, a convoy would only have one blimp assigned.

"My unit was ZP Squadron 14 out of Weeksville, North Carolina. After graduating from blimp training at Lakehurst, I was transferred to Weeksville. There were many other blimp stations along the eastern and Gulf coasts. Also, there were stations in Trinidad and Casablanca in North Africa, covering shipping in the

Mediterranean. We had enough fuel to fly for up to forty hours, or thirty hours at cruising speed.

"After hovering above the convoy, moving back and forth along the length of their column for twenty-four to thirty hours, we would be relieved by another blimp which would provide escort to the limit of our range. After exceeding our escort range limit, the convoy would begin to break down into groups of ships going to various European and English ports, moving in zig-zag courses. They were still escorted by the airplanes flying from the small carriers and the naval destroyers."

On Patrol

"One clear day we were patrolling out of Norfolk, Virginia, when we saw what appeared to be three cruisers. We did not have any notification or intelligence which said three cruisers would be in our area. They were plying abreast as we approached and began to attempt to make contact by radio. It was the French battleship, *Richelieu*, which had hidden itself by painting three cruisers on its side. If a sub had surfaced, they would have been deterred from attack because they would have seen cruisers, just as we had done. It was one ship camouflaged to look like three ships.

"Since I was trained as a metalsmith worker, I was responsible for aircraft maintenance. A major part of my duties while we were in the air was maintaining proper fuel flow and balance from the many tanks which were in the fueling system. Also, the engines had to be closely monitored. Each crew member took a turn at flying the left seat and controlling direction and course. The occupant of the right seat controlled the elevation. It required two pilots to handle the manual controls.

"As a metalsmith, I was often part of a group performing repairs on the many metal components on the airships. The huge fins, the ailerons, framing, and other parts were made of metal. Actually, a blimp has more metal in it than the standard fixed-wing aircraft.

"I remember one time in Weeksville when, during a storm, the wind blew a ship sideways into a hangar door and almost cut the main fin in half, disabling the craft. Another mechanic named Phillips and I were assigned to accomplish the repairs. We were given a stack of specifications and blueprints that was about two feet high. They wanted the ship back in service as quickly as possible, top priority. We worked eighteen to twenty hours per day, sleeping in short naps. We had it done ahead of schedule and received commendations from the base commander and our unit captain."

An Opportunity for a College Education

Through all of his earlier training in the military, Wayne had consistently demonstrated that he was an intelligent, quick-learning student. That attribute made him eligible for a unique educational program that was to change his life forever.

Wayne tells how it began. "In late 1943 the base commander called my friend Phillips and me to his office. He said, 'I have two positions for the Navy College V-12 Training Course, a full-time college assignment. Do you guys want them?' Completion of this course meant we would receive a commission and become naval officers. Of course, we accepted his offer.

"I was given a choice of where I wanted to go to school, and what courses I wanted to study. I opted for Columbia University and taking pre-med courses. Early in 1944 I was in New York and was enrolled as a full-time student on the Columbia campus. I attended classes with the regular Columbia students.

"I realized pretty quickly that, because I came from a small, rural school, I was somewhat at a disadvantage when competing with students who had been prepared in advanced programs in the New York school system. I lived in the regular student dormitories, Livingston Hall and others. I needed some assistance in trigonometry, since my high school did not have that subject and it was an absolute necessity at Columbia. I was tutored by another student named Murray Butter, who sort of took me under his wing and gave me a lot of assistance.

"I soon changed my course of study to engineering, partially because of problems I was having in language classes. The professor was difficult, and he said that Southerners couldn't speak French. Medical students had to have at least one foreign language. After encountering difficulties with French, I tried to learn German, but still found it difficult. Since engineering students did not have to have another language, I decided to switch to electrical engineering. After switching to engineering I felt I was heading in the right direction for my real interests and abilities.

"I recall taking a very difficult physics course for engineering, under Dr. Herman Farwell. One day, after leaving one of his lectures on the future uses of atomic energy, the likelihood of space stations, and space travel, my mind was absorbed in what he had said. As I walked down the stairway, I was so preoccupied that I went down one floor too far. When I reached the landing and opened the door out of the stairwell, I was immediately accosted by a couple of uniformed guards who gruffly asked, 'What are you doing here?' I told them I was trying to get back to my dormitory and had accidentally come down too far on the stairs. They promptly turned me around and ushered me back into the stairwell. I did not realize that I had walked into the area of the building where Dr. Farwell and others were working on the Manhattan Project.[4] At the time, I thought the topics of atomic energy and space which Farwell had discussed in class were 'Buck Rogers stuff' and many years away into the future, but in reality it was happening in our building.

"Frequently on Sunday afternoons, I would go downtown to Carnegie Hall to see Arturo Rodzinsky[5] and the New York Philharmonic. I felt that coming out of the sticks in Alabama I needed to absorb all of that Ivy League culture that I could find. This was a cultural opportunity for me, and I enjoyed it very much. I attended church at New York's Riverside Church where

Reverend Harry Emerson Fosdick was pastor. He was one of the premier theologians of that day."

Learning About Prejudices

"My schooling at Columbia was my first introduction to integrated classes and social association with members of the black race. Some of my best friendships which were cultivated at Columbia were with black students. I remember one of my closest black friends worked part-time at a nearby drugstore. I was addicted to milkshakes then (and still am). My friend made a lot of delicious shakes for me and we shared a lot of great conversations over his counter at the drugstore. He complimented me for my friendly, outgoing, southern personality.

"He and I had several conversations relating to racial relations, integration, and experiences. I told him that even though I was raised in a completely segregated South, I had never experienced a demonstration of prejudice while growing up. However only one black family lived within ten miles of our farm, and none worked on our farm or any neighboring farms.

"The one black man who lived near us at Mixson Corner was old Earnest Epson. My grandmother loved the old man and his wife and would chastise any who demeaned them in any way. She affectionately referred to him as 'Uncle Earnest.' That name was used in an endearing, respectful manner at that time.

"Because all schools were segregated in those days, I had little contact with any black youth while I was growing up. My first memory of black children was when the chorus at the all-black Vanderbilt Community School was invited to perform a program at the Elba High School while I was a student there. I knew as they sang 'We Are Climbing Jacob's Ladder' that their enthusiasm was lifting us all toward heaven. Their voices were angelic as they sang several spirituals. My impression of the group was that they were kind, respected God, and were very talented.

"I grew up knowing little about racial prejudices. There were no blacks in our schools and only two or three Jewish children. Sidney Orenson was in my high school class. I found him to be a good friend and a good student. The only differences that I noted was that he always had more money than I did, and he went to a different church.

"I first realized that prejudices existed regarding the Jewish population while I attended Columbia University in New York. When I showed a friend a picture of a girl I had started dating, he laughed and told me she was 'Jewish.' I was puzzled because I had never encountered that kind of prejudice.

"I found it unique that, even though I had been raised in South Alabama where it was assumed the Ku Klux Klan had great influence, I had not encountered racial prejudices until I went to New York. I can honestly say that during those years I never knew a Klan member, and my parents, who were also born and raised there, also stated they had never known one to their knowledge.

"Joe Louis, the great boxer, was born and raised in an adjoining Alabama county. We all followed his bouts on radio and were proud that he was from our area, We were especially supportive of him when he fought the German champion, Max Schmeling."[6]

On to Philadelphia and Penn State

"I was a pretty serious student in college. I was not rowdy, and never drank a single beer. In my family alcohol was strictly forbidden and that discipline remained with me through my Navy and college years. I regularly wrote letters home to my parents, and to Margie Grace, the beautiful young woman I had met from Graceville, Florida.

"I studied engineering at Columbia and Denison[7] for two years. When the studies turned to detailed design work involving extensive drafting, I began to lose some of my enthusiasm for the courses. Eventually I transferred to the University of Pennsylvania at the Wharton School to study business administration. Thus, my degrees actually resemble Industrial Engineering, with calculus, thermal dynamics, physics, and other science subjects, along with business and finance. It turned out to be a good combination.

"The University of Pennsylvania is located in Philadelphia, another large, northern city. I found the business courses I took there to be very interesting. Many of the classes at the Wharton School were audited by people from the business community for personal development, not for college credits. I recall one statement made by Dr. Dobeman, a noted professor at Wharton. He said, 'You are destined to be the future captains of industry. At times you may find that there is a general among you, but it will not be because he is here. Generals are born. However, your training here will assure your success at the intermediate level of business. To rise to the top requires more than scholastic training.' Because of that statement, I began to notice the backgrounds of many of our industrial leaders. I was astounded to find that many did not even have a high school diploma.

"I was a member of the Phi Gamma Delta fraternity while at the University of Pennsylvania, and still cherish some of the friendships I made there. Penn graduates from those years still gather for an annual reunion somewhere in Florida to recall fond memories from while we were in college.

"I was in advanced ROTC by this time and was destined to get my commission as a Navy officer. I was enrolled in Penn, attending classes, when the war ended. The celebration in downtown Philadelphia was almost as large as the one old films show in Times Square in New York. On campus, we built a huge bonfire in the quadrangle.

"V-J Day was August 5, and I had accumulated enough time to qualify for discharge. So at the end of the quarter in November, I applied for discharge. They tried to get me to stay in the Navy and become a commissioned officer, but I was ready to give up military life. I was transferred to Miami where the 'outgoing unit'

(OGU) was located, and after about ten days was sent to Jacksonville to be discharged. It was February of 1946.

"It was during this immediate post-war period when many of the men of my generation took advantage of their veterans' education benefits.8 They became doctors, lawyers, corporate executives, military leaders, college professionals, politicians, and even presidents. This explosion in the educational level of the population of America enabled the technological boom our nation enjoyed for the next fifty years. They had been seasoned by growing up during the Depression, tested by the trials of a great World War, and were prepared to participate in building the nation's economy to new heights. I am proud to be part of this generation of Americans.

"Many from my generation achieved success without an advanced education. Later in life I was discussing our generation with Senator George Aiken9 of Vermont. The senator often said, 'I'm just a little farm boy with a sixth-grade education.' That might have been the extent of his formal schooling, but his life experiences during the Depression and the war taught him well, as he often demonstrated during his thirty-four years as a senator. For many of those years he was chairman of the Senate Agricultural Committee.

"In the summer of 1946 I was enrolled at the University of Florida as a senior. Being a Gator and UF graduate was a benefit to me later in life while I was in politics. During that gap between my discharge and starting at UF, I taught math and sociology one semester as a student teacher at the Graceville High School. I was paid $75 per month. That experience deepened my appreciation and respect for schoolteachers for the rest of my life. Then I ended up marrying one."

The following year, 1947,10 Wayne graduated from the University of Florida with honors and a degree in Business Administration. Then he got his first job in industry with Bell Telephone inJacksonville, Florida, as an accountant. A new phase of Wayne's life was about to begin.

Endnotes

1. The Pea River is a scenic 154-mile-long (248 km) tributary of the Choctawhatchee River, which meanders through Coffee County near Mixson's Crossroads, Alabama. Local residents refer to the area as the "Pea River Valley."

2. In June 1940 Congress passed a Public Law for a 10,000-plane program, which included a provision for 48 non-rigid airships. When Japan bombed Pearl Harbor six months later the only airships in service were ten training airships. Only six (the K and TC types) were large enough for sea service, but the L-ship would be used for coastal patrol. The only operational base was at Lakehurst, New Jersey.

3. The Chief of Naval Operations (CNO) is a statutory office held by a four-star admiral in the United States Navy, and is the most senior naval officer assigned to serve in the Department of the Navy. As a member of the Joint Chiefs of Staff, the CNO is a military adviser to the National Security Council, the Homeland Security Council, the Secretary of Defense, and the president.

4. The Manhattan Project was a research and development project that produced the first nuclear weapons during World War II. During development of the atomic bomb, atomic research was underway at several of the nation's leading engineering schools.

5. Arturo Rodzinski (January 1, 1892-November 27, 1958) was a Polish conductor of opera and symphonic music. He is especially noted for his tenures as music director of the Cleveland Orchestra and the New York Philharmonic in the 1930s and 1940s.

6. Joe Louis vs. Max Schmeling refers to two separate fights between the two atheletes. Schmeling won the first match by a knockout in round twelve, but in the second match, Louis won through a knockout in the first round. The two fights came to embody the broader political and social conflict of the times. Louis was a focal point for African American pride in the 1930s. Moreover, as a contest between representatives of the United States and Nazi Germany, the fights came to symbolize the struggle between democracy and fascism. Louis's performance in the bouts therefore elevated him to the status of the first true black national hero in the United States.

7. "I transferred to Denison University in Ohio for my second college year. At Denison I began my major in Business. After two semesters at Denison, I was able to gain admission to the prestigious Wharton School of Business at the University of Pennsylvania."

8. About 16 million Americans served during WW II, and 72% of those veterans during the postwar era took advantage of VA educational benefits. Many had been places and seen things beyond what they ever could have imagined. The nation wanted to thank them for their service. One way Congress decided to do that became known as the G.I. Bill of Rights.

9. George David Aiken (August 20, 1892-November 19, 1984) was an American farmer and politician. A Republican, he was the 64th governor of Vermont (1937-1941) before serving in the United States Senate for 34 years, from 1941 to 1975. At the time of his retirement, he was the senior member of the Senate. Aiken was rooted in the state's progressive traditions, but distrusted any increase in presidential power.

10. 1947 was the first year that the University of Florida admitted women. Prior to that year it had been an all-male campus.

CHAPTER THREE

MARGIE GRACE MIXSON

Love at First Sight

The year was 1942. At this time Wayne was an active young man, approaching his prime. Immediately after he graduated from high school in the spring of 1941, he had taken a construction job in Panama City, Florida, and was living alone, away from the farm for the first time in his life. Most importantly, it was at this point that Margie Grace entered his life. They would never have met if Wayne's first cousin, French Mixson, had not married Margie's first cousin, Mary Clyde Grace. Another proof of the old adage, "God works in mysterious ways, His wonders to perform."

Wayne vividly remembers their first meeting. "I saw her for the first time on a spring morning in April. I had just graduated from New Brockton High School. I was working for a construction company in Panama City, Florida, which was engaged in a contract to help build Tyndall Air Force Base. Another of my cousins, Howard Lasseter, and I had rolled into Graceville, Florida, on our motorcycles. We were on our way from New Brockton to Panama City and had decided to stop for a visit with French and his new wife, who was teaching at Graceville High School. While we were standing and talking in the entrance hallway of Graceville High School, fourteen-year-old Margie Grace came up the school steps.

"I was immediately struck with her vibrant beauty. Mary Clyde called her over and introduced us. 'Miss Grace, this is Mr. Mixson.' Another student who was standing nearby said, 'She is my math teacher's daughter.' I didn't hear him say the word 'daughter' and thought the student had said that Margie was his math teacher. Margie already looked mature enough at that young age to be a teacher.

"My cousin and I spent most of the rest of that day fishing at a local lake. All through the day I could not keep from thinking of the beautiful girl I had met that morning, commenting about the 'cute, young math teacher' at Graceville. This confused French for a while. He knew that Margie's mother was a math teacher, but she was in her forties. Before the day was over, he realized that I was talking about Margie, and he corrected my perceptions. I was already so infatuated with her that when I realized how young she was, it almost ruined a good fishing trip.

"Mary Clyde and French, who lived next door to Margie and her parents, invited me to stay over at their house that night, They promised they would invite Margie to come over to play cards. That evening, after the games ended, I cleverly volunteered to walk the very young Margie Grace home. I put my arm around her for comfort since it was dark and kind of scary. Later, Margie described how nervous she was to be with a man who was five years older than her, and how I nearly scared her to death, since I was an 'older man.'"

The Grace Family

Margie Grace was born in the Baltzell Hospital[1] in Marianna, Florida, on July 12, 1927, the only child of George and Wilkie Bowen Grace. Margie has always been beautiful, even as a baby. "This is testified to by the fact that she was designated as the 'Prettiest Baby' at the 1929 Satsuma Festival in Marianna," Wayne brags as Margie blushes shyly.

When Margie was two years old, the Grace family moved from Marianna to Graceville, Florida, a small, vibrant town located in the northwestern area of Jackson County. The population of Graceville at that time was around 2,000. The town was recognized as a center for local agriculture, which produced peanuts, cotton, cattle, and watermelons.

The Grace family has deep roots in Graceville. The town was named for Margie's great-grandfather, Henry Bartlett Grace, who was a captain during the Civil War, and one of the early settlers and founders of the town. The Grace family's forefathers arrived in the New World from England around the same time that the early Mixson forefathers arrived, which was around 1650. The two families followed an almost identical migration inland. Margie's ancestor, Garrett Williams, first settled in Virginia, then went on to North Carolina, Georgia, and finally Alabama. Her great-great-grandfather arrived in Florida in the early 1800s, settling in Indian-inhabited territory that would soon become Jackson County. Margie's grandfather was born in 1861, the same year that the Civil War began. This resulted in his parents naming him Jefferson Davis Grace.

By the standards of the Depression era, Margie's parents were quite successful. Margie's mother was a 1920 graduate of Huntingdon College[2] in Montgomery, Alabama. After graduation she went to work as a high school teacher in Washington County. At that time, she was one of the few teachers in the area who held a four-year degree.

When Margie's father, George, went to school in Graceville, the school only provided instruction through the ninth grade. In order to finish high school, he had to be boarded twenty-five miles away in Marianna. He started teaching as soon as he graduated from high school. He taught for a short time and then enrolled at the University of Florida, where he graduated in the class of 1912.[3] He immediately started teaching and worked for years as an educator, except for a time when he served as the U.S. Consul to the Azores Islands during World War I. He was later elected as the Jackson County Superintendent of Schools.

Both of Margie's parents were teachers and vigorous proponents of education. They felt that travel was a useful means of educating children, so Margie and her family went on many summer trips during Margie's formative years. The experience gained from this early travel created an unquenchable appetite for travel that she has enjoyed throughout her life. In 1937, when she was ten, they planned a journey which would take Margie across the mighty Mississippi River for the first time. On the way, they visited Pensacola, New Orleans, and Baton Rouge.

In New Orleans she saw, for the first time, Catholic priests and nuns on the streets wearing their church vestments. This was notable to her since there were no Catholics living in Graceville at the time. In fact, there may have also been no members of the Jewish faith living there. When Margie inquired about their vestments, her father told her, "Oh, they are Catholics." From that, ten-year-old Margie assumed all Catholics dressed in that manner. Several years later, when she met someone who said he was a Catholic, Margie replied, "Oh! You don't look like one!"

On that same trip her family visited the top of the Louisiana State Capitol Building in Baton Rouge. She became frightened when she looked over the edge of the building and has had to frequently overcome an aversion to heights ever since. The highlight of this trip came during the time the family spent in Pensacola. Margie's father had planned their visit to coincide with an event which President Roosevelt was scheduled to attend. She recalls how thrilled she was to stand on a sidewalk and wave as the president passed by in an open car.

Margie's family had another of these memorable excursions two years later, when she was twelve years old. Margie, her mother, and some other ladies went to New York City to the 1939 World's Fair. On the way they made a scheduled stop in Washington, D.C. On the day they were there, King George and Queen Elizabeth of

England were visiting with President and Eleanor Roosevelt. Once again, Margie had the thrill of standing on the sidewalk as their procession passed by in open cars. For a twelve-year-old student from rural Graceville, Florida, it was an unforgettable moment.

Margie recalls, "I am sure that this was a very important meeting for these two world leaders since the year was 1939 and England was facing the growing aggression of Germany and Adolf Hitler. It was a time of planning, development of strategies, and strengthening of alliances between America and England.

"New York and the World's Fair were also unforgettable experiences for me. I had never experienced so many people, so many tall buildings, and the wonders of the fair. However, when people asked me what the most memorable thing was I saw on that trip, I always said that the most memorable occasion on the trip for me was my first-time viewing of television. It seemed to be unbelievable that live images could be transmitted for miles through the airways." It was to be many years later before television came to Graceville.

Both of these trips were fantastic learning experiences for Margie, but the family excursion she apparently remembers most vividly was the trip the family took in 1941, when she was fourteen. They drove across the southern part of the United States, stopping to visit relatives in Texas and then dipping down to the border town of Juarez so they could say they had visited Mexico. Then it was westward to southern California and a thrilling drive northward up California's rugged coastline, then Oregon and Washington, and finally crossing into Canada at Vancouver so they could claim they had visited Canada. From there they headed southeast, moving diagonally across the country. They passed the Grand Tetons in Wyoming and the Petrified Forest and Grand Canyon in Arizona, and finally reached Florida and home. It was a giant circle that covered a big portion of the United States, with visits to Mexico and Canada. Quite a trip in 1941!

43

The endless plains, cactus-filled deserts, majestic mountains, awe-inspiring coastlines, and endless varieties of towns, communities, and cities implanted a realization of how varied and huge our nation was. Margie saw how Florida had its own beauty and unique topography and was just one part of the huge national mosaic.

Another trip was planned for two years later, in 1943. However, by this time the world was engulfed in a horrible war. Gasoline was rationed, the nation was focused on winning the war, and travel for pleasure was out of the question. Margie's next era of travel was to occur with Wayne, as they shared their public lives and the opportunities which were to come.

"Together we traveled the world, visiting many beautiful, wonderful places. Some of these trips were on official government business, while other trips were personal pleasure trips. The places where I accompanied Wayne included China, Japan, Korea, Australia, New Zealand, Africa, India, Nepal, Russia, Norway, Sweden, Denmark, Spain, Portugal, Germany, Italy, Belgium, Ireland, Holland, Israel, and Scotland. My favorite country was England," Margie recalls.

Continuing the Relationship

A few weeks after that first introduction to Wayne, Margie and her family were next door visiting the Mixsons, sitting on their front porch, enjoying a beautiful Easter Sunday afternoon. While they were visiting, Wayne and his cousin stopped their car in front of the house. Wayne's cousin was with a date, and they were all planning to go for an afternoon ride. Wayne invited Margie to join the group.

Young Margie was hesitant about going, and her mother also had some reservations. Once again, it was their first cousins, French and Mary Clyde, who saved the day for them. Since they were next door neighbors and relatives, Margie's mother didn't want to offend them, so she reluctantly agreed to let Margie go.

They drove the fifteen miles to Marianna, toured around town, and then drove out across the countryside. Wayne recalls, "I was wearing my Easter suit, and she looked stunning in an unforgettable polka dot dress. I have and still cherish a picture which was taken that day. It shows a beautiful, young Margie standing alongside the road, smiling her winning smile, wearing that dress. The picture was taken while we stopped along the road to look at some cattle. It was at that moment, while admiring her stunning beauty and great personality, that I said to myself, 'Someday I am going to ask that girl to marry me!' Little did I dream that I would also make her Florida's First Lady. My decision that day to eventually marry Margie Grace was the best decision I was to make in my entire life. Another wonderful blessing from God.

"Within a few months I was enlisted in the Navy, mustering through training, and finally on active duty engaging in blimp patrol assignments. I came home on leave every few months, and always spent as much time as I could with Margie. As long as she was in high school, her mother insisted that we always double-dated. So, when I arranged a date with Margie, I also had to find another couple to go with us. I was separated from Margie for almost four years during the war, but we corresponded once or twice per week. Margie says it was those letters that made her fall in love with me. We still have four suitcases filled with our letters that chronicle our courtship and growing love."

Margie Starts College

While Wayne was away up north serving in the Navy, Margie graduated from Graceville High School as valedictorian of her class. She was awarded the Lewis Scholarship[4] at Florida State University for Women in Tallahassee and began her college work there.

Initially Margie was not sure what she wanted as her college major. Her mother, Wilkie, suggested, "You will probably be married some day and you will need homemaking skills, so why don't you major in Home Economics?" With that encouragement,

Margie entered that field of studies, and it ended up being a terrible choice for her. By the end of her freshman year, she was so discouraged that she even considered dropping out. Fortunately, this situation was corrected when she visited her guidance counselor, Dean Eymen, who asked her "What class do you most enjoy?"

"English," Margie answered.

"Then why don't you major in English?"

Margie followed the advice, and soon realized that her interest in school was restored. This led to a degree in Education, with a major in English. She joined the Delta Zeta sorority and was invited into the Phi Kappa Phi[5] Honor Society. This enabled her wonderful career as a high school teacher and community college teacher. She ended up teaching English in six Florida high schools and finally at Chipola Junior College. Her teaching career spanned thirty years, the last twelve at Chipola in Marianna.

After the war ended, the couple was still forced to be apart, since Margie was still going to college in Tallahassee and Wayne was in Gainesville, finishing his senior year at the University of Florida.

Margie claims that as a young girl she had decided she did not want to marry a farmer. She said they usually were covered in dirt from the fields and were rough from all of the hard labor. When she makes that statement in public, Wayne always responds with, "We farmers didn't like those pointed-headed, briefcase-toting, businessmen, either!"

There were significant differences between the formative years and family environment for Margie and Wayne. Margie was an only child, while Wayne was one of three children. Wayne's mother and father had adequate educations for the time, while George and Wilkie Grace were educators with more advanced learning. Her father was elected the county school superintendent and later owned an insurance business. Her mother was a teacher and became assistant school principal. Ironically, in her classes, her mother would usually skip the course content dealing with income taxes. She claimed that none of the students would ever make enough to have to pay taxes. How times have changed!

Margie's maternal grandfather, James Thomas Bowen, who had seven children, was also a schoolteacher. He once told his children, "I am not going to leave you any money when I die. However, I will provide as much education as you can take." Margie's mother was the oldest child and was the first of the children to graduate from college. She graduated the same year that women in the United States were given the right to vote, 1920. All seven of the children attended college, so the legacy served its intended purpose.

Back in those days you could go to college for two years and obtain an L1 diploma, which certified you as a teacher. It was very rare for a teacher in elementary or high school to have a four-year degree. Margie was among the few who did.

Margie's father, George Grace, was superintendent of schools in Jackson County from 1925 through 1928, and his picture adorns the wall of the entrance foyer in the school board building. His picture was hung in a formal ceremony in 2009 by the then-current superintendent of schools, Lee Miller, who was also from Graceville. The occasion honored George Grace and his daughter, Margie. Superintendent Miller remarked about how much Margie had helped him while he was a student at Chipola College and Margie was a Chipola instructor.

"I Thee Wed"

Wayne always smiles peacefully as he tells the story of his proposal and marriage to Margie Grace. "I proposed to Margie on a beautiful Fourth of July evening in 1946 as we strolled on the white sands of Panama City Beach. It was a tradition for Margie's family to rent a cottage at Panama City Beach at this time each year, and I had joined them for the holiday. We managed to leave the crowd for a walk on the beach. I seized the opportunity to propose to her. I was blessed when she accepted.

47

"Since at that time I was finishing my last year at the University of Florida, and she was attending Florida State, our initial plans were for us to remain engaged until we had both finished college, which would have been during the summer of 1948. However, those plans were changed when it worked out that I was going to go to work for AT&T in Jacksonville after I graduated in the spring of 1947. Margie initially worked out a plan to finish her required internship by teaching for three months at a school in Jacksonville, then returning to Tallahassee to finish her studies and graduate in 1948. Her mother soon realized that plan would place us both in Jacksonville, still unmarried, so she refused to allow Margie to go to Jacksonville unless we were married.

"Margie and I were married on December 27, 1947, at the Graceville Methodist Church. It was the best Christmas of my life! By chance, we have some close friends who were married on the same date and year, so we always get with them for a joint celebration at the Governor's Club in Tallahassee. On our wedding day, Margie and her father walked arm-in-arm. Beginning at their house, their walk covered the block from their home to the church. Margie didn't want to ride in a car and take a chance the ride might crinkle her magnificent dress.

"It was a beautiful, star-filled night for the reception, which was held at the Grace home. Our wedding celebration was a big event for little Graceville at the time. The local banker and some of his friends fitted up the car we used on our honeymoon. When we cranked the car, it ignited smoke bombs and firecrackers. Then as we drove away, we drug a long string of cow bells. Our lifelong journey together had begun with a bang.

"Neither of us had a car at that time. We appreciated Margie's grandmother providing her car for us to use on our honeymoon. We drove to Panama City's Cove Hotel for our first night together."

Margie finished her college courses and graduated from FSU the following year in June of 1948. This launched a thirty-year career in education for her, teaching English in six Florida high schools and finally at Chipola Junior College. She was later to earn her Masters Degree in Education from the University of Florida . . . so they both have degrees from that fine Florida school.

In the 1947 school year the name of her college was changed from the Florida State College for Women to Florida State University, and the campus became coeducational.[6] With college now behind both of them and Wayne employed by the telephone company in Jacksonville, they planned to set up a household in Jacksonville as they both began their promising careers; except Wayne had developed another itch!

Endnotes

1. The Baltzell Hospital was owned and operated by the popular Jackson County physician, Dr. Nicholas Baltzell. The fifteen-room hospital was opened in 1913. It also included a colored ward. The facility was located on the main street in Marianna, Florida, on the corner of Lafayette Street (Highway 90) and Russ Street.

2. Huntingdon College, founded in 1854, was a women's liberal arts college affiliated with the United Methodist Church in Montgomery, Alabama. Huntingdon College was chartered on February 2, 1854, as Tuskegee Female College by the Alabama State Legislature and Governor John A. Winston. Today it is coeducational.

3. At that time the entire student enrollment at the University of Florida was 200 students.

4. This was a scholarship named for State Senator Lewis from Marianna. It was only for prospective teachers entering Florida schools.

5. The Honor Society of Phi Kappa Phi was established in 1897 to recognize superior scholarship for all areas of study, and to promote the "unity and democracy of education." Its mission is "to recognize and promote academic excellence in all fields of higher education and to engage the community of scholars in service to others."

6. Due to the sudden and extreme increase in the need for college space for the men who were returning from World War II and using the G.I. Bill for education benefits, several women's colleges across the nation became coeducational during the immediate post-war era.

CHAPTER FOUR

TWENTY YEARS IN THE PRIVATE SECTOR

Back to the Farm

The winding pathway of life is filled with twists, turns, and forks in the road. When arriving at one of these forks, the traveler must make a decision. Usually it is a decision that will dramatically impact the remainder of his or her life. For most of us, one of the most important of these decisions is the choice of a career.

In 1947, shortly after graduating from the University of Florida, Wayne moved to Jacksonville, Florida, where he went to work for Southern Bell Telephone Company as an accountant. Wayne recalls how he struggled with a life-changing decision. "I enjoyed my work as an accountant, and the company had already promoted me to a position with greater responsibilities. We had planned that when Margie graduated from FSU in the spring of 1948, she would join me in Jacksonville to set up our first home.

"However, there was a nagging problem! I had developed a sincere desire to return to farming as my career, instead of becoming an accountant! After working for less than a year in the business world, I realized that I really wanted to be a farmer. I guess it was just in my blood. When I left home after high school in 1941, my father owned a small, 160-acre farm. By 1946 he had accumulated some 1,200 acres and an impressive armada of tractors and equipment. In the postwar era, the world was very hungry, and farming was replete with opportunity. Land values were still depressed, and farming technology was exploding. I felt my potential for succeeding was much better as a farmer. My instincts told me that the time was right for the American farmer. Land was cheap and the new technologies were exciting. Even though Southern Bell was a fine company, I no longer wanted to work as an accountant! I decided to resign and head back to Jackson County.

"It was time for spring planting and I had definitely decided city life and the corporate world was not the career I wanted. My mother and father had recently moved to Florida after they bought a farm in Jackson County, near Campbellton. One of Dad's brothers had also relocated to Jackson County. My father had always felt the soil in the Florida panhandle was superior to the soil on our Alabama homestead. Because of these factors, when a sizable tract of land came available near Campbellton, he decided to sell out in Alabama and move to Florida. This was a major decision for him that probably resulted in me becoming a Florida citizen.

"I phoned my dad and asked him to find some land in the area that I could rent. He told me that he had an extra tractor he could lend me until we could buy our own. I made the decision to change career paths at that time, a major step in our life-journey. So the pathway was now open; I was returning to the land.

"Margie cried when I broke the news to her. She was prepared to live a city life, and suddenly she found herself going back to Jackson County as a farmer's wife. Although I had grown up on a farm, I had never studied agriculture, and she had some reservations about our potential for success. Nevertheless, always the trouper standing at my side, she agreed to go along, as we took this new direction together."

Jackson County Farmer, Wayne Mixson

At this point Wayne's love affair with Jackson County, Florida, began. Margie and Wayne initially rented an apartment in Graceville. They were now located near both of their parents. Wayne's mother and father had a new home and farm outside of Campbellton, Florida, and Margie's family still lived in Graceville. Wayne found the lifestyle, local infrastructure, attitudes of the people, and good ole southern country living of the area to be identical to the environment in which he had been raised in southern Alabama. Unlike most children of their era, who were leaving farms for city life, Wayne and Margie had returned to their roots.

Soon Wayne was out in the hot, dusty fields driving a tractor, and Margie was teaching, first in Campbellton and then in Graceville. They bought a 170-acre farm for a whopping $22 per acre, along with a new tractor. While they were able to live off Margie's $2,400-a-year teaching salary, the crop revenues that first year paid for the land and the tractor. During the next few years, they continued to buy land since it was so inexpensive and productive. Wayne's main interest was cattle, so he began to also build a cattle herd.

The impact that the new technologies were having on farm productivity was astounding. Wayne recalls these changes, "My father and I had always been eager to accept new farm technology as it came to the market. He brought the first tractor with rubber tires to Coffee County, Alabama, at his farm at Mixson Crossroads. Now, he and I together were among the first farmers in Jackson County to buy and begin using the new peanut combine which had just been invented. I could see that the industrial revolution was rapidly impacting the agricultural industries in the postwar era. With the large tractors and new accessory equipment which we had begun to use on our farms, we were only taking two to three hours per acre to harvest peanuts when it had previously required forty-four hours of manual labor. The world was hungry, and we were gearing up to help feed it.

"The first big farm I bought was 700 acres, which had previously provided a living for more than a dozen families when mules were used. Now I was running that same farm with only four men. Through similar modernization on my father's farm, twenty-three families had been uprooted. Mr. Burton, who was the head of the extension service in Georgia, once told me that in the ten years spanning the 1950s and 1960s, over 100,000 people in the ten southwest Georgia counties had been forced to move to Albany, Atlanta, or somewhere else in order to find a job. This realization of the problems that technology had created for those fine families was to have a profound impact on me during my entire legislative career."

It was during this time that farming became a real business. Previously, with the small farm units, low land values, lack of mechanization, and relatively poor housing, a farm had few capital assets. As a result, there were few banking opportunities for a farmer when he needed financing.

With mechanization these small family farms were consolidated, expensive machinery came into use, farming productivity exploded, cost of land increased, and thus, large capital investments were required. Farming became a well-financed business venture. As land values began to rise rapidly, bankers began to seek out farm loans, since these commercial loans were usually larger than most city retail accounts. Farms grew larger and larger as more consolidations took place, and the small family farms disappeared. At the turn of the century, more than half of the U.S. population lived on farms. By the end of the century, that number had dropped to under five percent of the population still residing on farms; the rest had migrated to the cities.

Farmers Also Needed Telephones

As a farmer, Wayne soon became an active member of the local Farm Bureau, and began to be involved in the promotion of local farm interests. As a result of his active participation, he was elected president of the Jackson County Farm Bureau. During his term as president, he led a determined effort to get telephone service run into the county's rural areas. At that time there were almost no telephones located outside of an urban area anywhere in North Florida. The telephone companies had decided that the population density in rural areas was too sparse for service to be economically justified.

Wayne recalls fighting this battle for telephones. "Since we could get no meaningful response from Bell Telephone Company, we decided to take action on our own. Our countywide group took options on two small telephone companies located in Cottondale and Sneads and made plans to borrow funds from Rural Electric Corporation to build a rural system covering three counties. At first, they wanted us to demonstrate the market by obtaining two hundred paid and committed customers for the new system. We soon fulfilled this requirement and the project proceeded. After our loan request was approved, the major phone companies realized we were serious, and a new competitor was being created on their doorstep.

"The telephone companies did not want to see a rural co-op telephone company in their market area. As a result, each of these existing carriers promised to extend service to the hundreds of rural applicants we had in hand. They then proceeded rapidly to consolidate and build the rural system to our satisfaction. From this outcome we had learned the fact that sometimes you do not have to take 'no' as an answer. Meanwhile, AT&T had learned that they were not in total control.

"While President of the local Farm Bureau, I had also initiated an aggressive membership drive. As a result, the Jackson County District ended up with the largest membership of any county in Florida. We had more than doubled our number of active members. This success so impressed the Farm Bureau officials that in 1954 I was asked to assist in the organization of farmers in several other Florida counties. Thus, as a second job, I went to work with Florida Farm Bureau and with the American Farm Federation in membership recruitment for several years. I also continued to operate my farm in Jackson County. By this time, I had a dependable manager working at the farm, and it did not require my full-time attention."

During these busy years, Margie had begun to teach in Winter Park and in Gainesville. Because of these changes in their work routines, they decided that it would be more convenient if they moved to Tallahassee. Margie began to teach in Tallahassee, and Wayne regularly commuted between their Jackson County farm and the Farm Bureau headquarters in Winter Park. Commuting was not an easy task in those days since it was before interstate travel. Thus, in order to make their lives more convenient, the Mixsons moved to Tallahassee. Through his role with Farm Bureau's recruitment activity during these years, Wayne became acquainted with most of the agricultural leaders and politicians across the state. These relationships were to be invaluable in future years.

In 1958 upper management of American Farm Bureau offered Wayne a position as a program director for thirteen southern states and Puerto Rico. This was a top-level position in their organization. An important part of his new duties was to assist these states with their legislative programs. He assisted several southern states with drafting new agriculture-related legislation and then presenting it to legislative committees. As a result of these political activities, Wayne began to learn the inner procedures of state government. Also, this new job required him to attend many receptions and committee meetings with the state managers for Farm Bureau. Often these agricultural proposals involved national legislation, requiring him to work in Washington, D.C. The work was very interesting, but it was also very tiring. Wayne's horizons were broadening to national and international levels.

Wayne describes some of the personal problems that came with this new role. "This job involved almost continual travel, and I soon grew to detest airports and the buzz of airplanes. Once per month I had to travel out of Jacksonville to Chicago for a review meeting. Many of the engagements involved dinner and a cocktail hour, and since I did not drink, I was often bored. After only eight months of this lifestyle, I resigned and returned to the farm again."

In the early 1960s Wayne and Margie suffered three deeply felt losses. Wayne describes the events: "My beloved father died in 1962, and a few months later, in 1963, my wonderful mother also passed. He had always been a heavy smoker, and as his health failed, he died from a heart attack. Mother had always endured a weakened heart caused by undulant fever[1] when she was a young girl. She finally died as the result of her heart condition. On top of these losses, the following year Margie's father also passed. That was a difficult time for both of us since both families had always been so involved and supportive in our lives. We lovingly helped each other endure the grief.

"After my parents were gone, I managed the combined farms, which included the land my parents had owned and the land I had accumulated. Our landholdings would finally peak at over 2,000 acres. In 1966 we left Tallahassee and moved back to Marianna. We bought a home on Nolan Street and later another home in a nearby subdivision, Country Club Hills. Our house was near the entrance to Caverns State Park.

"At this time, Margie had begun to teach English at Chipola Junior College, back in Jackson County. Meanwhile, I operated the farm and continued to promote local, state, and national agricultural interests through Farm Bureau. Both of us had developed meaningful, productive careers."

It was at this point Wayne had his first encounter with Florida politics. He had developed a friendship with Dan McCarthy,[2] a World War II hero, a conservative Democratic legislator, and former speaker of the Florida House. McCarthy had made a strong, positive impression on Wayne. He agreed with his conservative message, respected his record, and felt that McCarthy could do a good job representing North Florida's interest as governor. As a result, Wayne agreed to be an active volunteer to assist him in his 1952 campaign for governor.

Wayne relates his role in this political work: "While Dan was campaigning in North Florida, the two of us traveled to all of the small towns in Washington, Holmes, and Jackson counties. I was one of the few fellows he had posted in this area during his primary race. Dan and I had a lot in common. During our travels together, we talked a lot about farm issues, growing up in the rural South during the Depression, the war, current issues, and campaign strategies. He had seen more actual combat than me during the war. Dan had been awarded a Bronze Star and a Purple Heart, along with many other campaign achievement ribbons.

"After the war, we had both graduated from the University of Florida and both had farming backgrounds. We enjoyed discussing the four major transitions we had seen in farming during our lifetimes. These were the electrification of farms, the paving of rural roads, mechanization of farming, and the installation of the telephone.

"Dan McCarthy was victorious and became the 31st governor of Florida in January 1953. Then he unfortunately died in September of that same year, at the age of forty-one. He had been a heavy smoker most of his life and was not in good health. I have always felt that he would have accomplished much for our state if he had lived to serve.

"After Dan's unfortunate death, I became active in helping Leroy Collins as he campaigned to become Dan's successor as governor. I even drove a sound truck for rallies in several West Florida counties, making music and calling people on the streets to come to his outdoor speeches. It was fun, but not too interesting as a job."

By the early 1960s Wayne had developed a sizable beef herd, and was very active in the beef market. He began a feedlot operation at the farm and became one of only four such operations in the state. Wayne explains, "As part of the strategy for the beef program we grew enough irrigated corn to supply grain for the fed cattle. We always provided a top grade of beef, feeding the cattle until they reached USDA Choice grade. Most of our fed cattle were sold to Central Packing Company in Sumter County, Florida. Among their customers was the U.S. Air Force at MacDill Field in Tampa, which was a major purchaser of the high-grade beef that only a few Florida farmers were producing. With the combined results of our significant beef business, and regular peanut and cotton production, our farm was doing a booming business."

Because of the continuing consolidation of many small family farms into large farming operations, and because of the steady development of technological improvements, by the 1960s agriculture had become a profession requiring both good business skills and lots of farming experience. The agricultural industries had become a meaningful part of the American economy. Wayne's early farming experiences, combined with his business education, enabled him to become a modern, professional farmer. However, Wayne Mixson was to demonstrate that he possessed career potential far beyond what he had already accomplished in business.

Endnotes

1. Undulant fever is a condition caused by a bacteria which thrives in raw milk. During the early 1920s milk was not pasteurized or homogenized to remove such bacteria. This bacteria can affect organs, including the heart.

2. Daniel Thomas "Dan" McCarthy (January 18, 1912–September 28, 1953). McCarthy was elected to the Florida House of Representatives and served as its speaker, and was later elected the 31st governor of Florida. On February 25, 1953, shortly after assuming the governorship, he suffered a debilitating heart attack and died on September 28, 1953, in Tallahassee. Dan McCarthy Middle School in St. Lucie County was named in his honor.

CHAPTER FIVE

WAYNE BEGINS HIS POLITICAL CAREER
From Farming to Politics

The year was 1966, and Wayne Mixson was now uniquely prepared to start the next phase of his life. He had behind him the early experiences of being a child of the Depression, being raised on a small, rural family farm in a loving family where a strong Christian foundation and good work ethic were instilled, he had worked early in life as a blue-collar worker, he had served distinctively in World War II, he had earned advanced degrees from some of the best colleges in America, he had experienced urban living in northern cities, he was married to a wonderful woman, he had over twenty successful years in agribusiness, he had worked with several state legislatures in drafting farm legislation as an executive with Farm Bureau, and Wayne Mixson was widely recognized and respected as one of the leaders in Florida's important agriculture industry. Few men have ever been better qualified for the job when they entered politics.

Wayne continues, "It seemed natural for my interest to eventually turn to politics. In my ancestry, my family on both sides was filled with men who had taken active political roles during their lives. In my lineage there were county judges, county officials, and state legislators, some of whom became widely known during their era. My great-grandfather, Goppa Tolmilge, once entered and passed a resolution in the Alabama legislature to negotiate with the state of Florida for the transfer of all land west of the Apalachicola River away from Florida into the State of Alabama.

"He was then appointed to lead a delegation to negotiate with the Florida government to accomplish this goal. After generating much interest and holding several negotiation sessions, the impending war between the northern and southern states caused the annexation effort to be discontinued. Additional efforts by Alabama legislators to reopen this issue after the end of the war also failed.

"While I was employed with the American Farm Bureau, I worked directly with many state organizations in their respective legislatures and in the federal Congress, promoting bills that were favorable to agriculture. From this exposure I felt that I was well prepared with knowledge and experience to opt for a seat in the state legislature in Florida."

A Changing World

Wayne had witnessed the rapid growth and mechanization of the farming industries, the transition as many small family farms were consolidated into fewer large farms, and the social hardships these changes had caused the thousands of farm laborers and their families. Wayne had a deep awareness of the fact that these changes had caused thousands of farm workers and sharecroppers to be displaced. Most of these families had been forced to move to northern urban areas in order to find a means of supporting their needs. Wayne had always felt a deep sadness for their plight and the disruption to their lives. Many of those who were impacted had been forced to sell small farms which had been in their families for generations. Wayne wanted to do something to help those people.

Another factor which helped spur the agricultural sector's rapid acceptance of new technologies was the implementation of a national minimum wage. As part of Roosevelt's recovery programs, in 1938 the first federal minimum was established at $0.25 per hour ($4.23 in 2015 dollars), with time-and-a-half paid for overtime. This added cost was potentially a crushing requirement to many struggling farmers, and labor-saving mechanization offered a solution. A fixed, single minimum wage also denied businesses and farms of the South a potential advantage they could have realized from the existing lower cost of living there, when compared to living in the North.

"I felt that government should work to help citizens who were negatively impacted by a large demographic transition, such as what was occurring in agriculture. To me it appeared that the obvious solution was to attract industries to come to our area and thus create good-paying industrial jobs for Florida's displaced agricultural workers," Wayne declares. "I wanted to help make those new jobs a reality."

The economy of the "Old South" was primarily dependent on agricultural commerce, especially cotton, which was shipped to textile mills in the North. There was very little industry throughout the southern agricultural areas. That condition was a result of the fact that Britain controlled the cotton and textile industries during the early era of development for our nation. After the Revolutionary War, many new textile mills were built in the Northeast. Most of these mills still regarded England as their primary market. The system was to grow it in the South, ship the cotton north to convert to cloth in the northern mills, and then ship the cloth to England.

During the era after World War II most of these Northern textile mills were becoming aged, with old buildings and old technology. When these large textile companies decided it was time to replace the old mills, they found a ready, non-union, lower-cost, trainable, and eager labor force in the southern states. Additionally, there was a freight cost advantage to having the mills located closer to the growing areas. This change also enhanced the development of southern ports.

By the end of World War II, the United States had undergone dramatic changes. In all industries, including agriculture, new technologies were lowering costs and increasing output. The U.S. market was expanding exponentially, on the way to becoming the world's largest market and economy. The labor force was becoming much better educated and had been matured by the world experiences gained while serving in the armed forces. Many of the skills they acquired while in the military were easily transferred to industrial applications.

The farmer was eager to trade his mules for a new tractor. New construction in industry and housing was spreading through the southern states. The trainable labor force in the South soon began building a wide variety of products which had previously only been manufactured in the North. Throughout the South job opportunities increased, the standard of living improved, and a sense of growing prosperity existed. In many areas, farmland was being converted into subdivisions and industrial parks.

Helping Cities, Farming, and Industry While Protecting Florida's Environment

State government in Florida was traditionally focused primarily on developing tourism and had few incentives to offer these job-producing industries that were seeking a southern location. Wayne felt this shortfall was a serious fault in legislative philosophy. He felt state programs creating industrial development incentives were direly needed. The need for these political changes continued to haunt him. It was developing into another one of those "itches" that usually plagued him to action.

Wayne recalls, "I thought to myself, 'There is much that needs to be done to help the state, to bring jobs to Florida, and to help cultivate our agricultural industries. I am qualified to accomplish what needs to be changed.' After deliberation, I decided to run for a state office.

"My home political district was an area where I was well known from my years of working with the local Farm Bureau as president, and then as a vice president of the Florida Farm Bureau in the position of director of organization. This role put me into direct contact with local field offices across the state as we developed and implemented agricultural programs. The job also included bringing several new counties into the Farm Bureau organization. It was my hope that those personal contacts would help me win a seat in the legislature.

"An important element of my work with Farm Bureau was assisting the field offices in bringing in new members, developing and distributing educational materials, and identification of agriculture-related issues which required legislative action at the local, state, and national levels. The local Farm Bureau organization at all levels was comprised of farmers who volunteered to serve as officers. It is a true 'grassroots' organization."

Today farming requires a tremendous amount of capital investment. Land has become expensive and meaningful farming requires an array of very expensive specialized equipment. Additionally, fertilizers, seeds, irrigation, and other ingredients of a crop are a major annual cost. These costs normally require the farmer to engage in important transactions with banks, insurance companies, and transportation systems. The tasks related to harvesting, processing, and marketing of products require specialized knowledge and skills. The combined impact of all of these elements of today's modern farming makes agriculture a huge multiplier of jobs, both on and away from the farm. Wayne was keenly aware of the importance of agribusiness to the Florida economy. Agriculture remains an important economic element of the economy in virtually every county in Florida.

Wayne continues, "In our urban areas, I had seen firsthand that conflicts of interest were arising between ongoing commercial and residential development and expanding agricultural needs. Fanning requires large amounts of land, consumes needed water, and our subtropical climate demands use of chemicals. Florida's legislators had to seek reasonable compromises between these conflicting needs to enable both activities to proceed.

"Much time and investment have been spent on research to develop improved practices in farming in order to enable compliance with environmental needs and coexistence with populated areas. I was convinced that there was enough room in Florida for agriculture, environmental protection, and urban growth to all flourish simultaneously. I wanted to work as a legislator during this era of change, assuring that agribusiness was respected. I wanted the opportunity to exercise a role in making the decisions which accomplished this goal. I knew that my upbringing on a farm, my role as an active farmer, and my years of work with Farm Bureau had endowed me with a unique level of experience and perspective for a Florida legislator.

"I also felt that creating new industrial jobs for Florida's growing labor force was necessary. The opportunity to bring these messages to the legislature and the managers of the state's counties and cities in Florida was an inviting challenge for me. It was apparent that the state was suffering from growing underemployment and unemployment. I felt that state government could play a vital role in the education and training of the labor force for new industries, and simultaneously could provide job opportunities through assisting in bringing new industries into areas of need. I was ready to work diligently to accomplish improvements in these areas in any future legislative role I might have. The presence of all of these growing needs is what motivated me to enter politics," Wayne proclaims.

The Reapportionment of 1966

In the fall of 1966 Wayne decided to qualify to run for the state senate seat which was being vacated by Senator Robert Williams of Graceville. Robert had taken a job as a division director in the Department of State. His district included Jackson, Holmes, and Washington Counties.

Immediately after Wayne officially filed for the seat, the federal Supreme Court suddenly changed the game for him. They mandated that the results of the statewide 1966 Florida elections be thrown out, and that all districts be reapportioned into an approved form which better represented the "one man, one vote" concept. This meant that Wayne's district had to be redesigned, and he had already paid his filing fees.

When the redesign was finished and approved, the new district design created a situation in which Wayne was competing against two incumbent senators for the seat, and the land area was vastly changed from what it had previously been. Instead of consisting of three local counties where Wayne was very popular, it now covered counties all the way to Jacksonville and down to St. Augustine. Initially he began to entertain the thought of withdrawing. Understandably, he was certainly disheartened.

After consideration, he did not withdraw, but he might as well have. In disgust, he put no effort into launching a campaign, spent no money on campaigning, and attended no campaign events. His friends had persuaded him to leave his name in the primary, knowing that a new opportunity to serve was coming soon and this initial exposure would be helpful. Even with the lack of competitive effort for the new senate seat, Wayne was pleased when he made a very respectful showing in the final election results. Mixson finished second in the race, beating one of the incumbents. He did not count it as a defeat, only as a learning experience.

Within a few days after this initial learning experience, a special election was called for the state representative seat in Wayne's local district. The redesigned house district included the counties of Gadsden, Liberty, and Jackson. Wayne was well known in all three counties. He was about to jump back into the game of politics.

The Morning "Mark Out Coffee Club"[1]

Every morning during the work week in Marianna, there is a meeting of a large coffee club group at one of the Marianna restaurants. This group is a mixture of many of the leading businessmen, retailers, city and county politicians, bureaucrats, and retirees in the community. Wayne occasionally enjoyed a morning cup of coffee with them.

On one of those occasions the conversation was directed toward the upcoming special election for state representative which was scheduled for early February. The coffee group earnestly urged Wayne to qualify and run for the open seat. They even generously offered to take up a collection among their group to pay the qualifying fee. Wayne graciously thanked them for their kind offer and support but declined their willingness to pay his fee. However, the discussion with them that morning did further ignite an ember of interest that had been smoldering inside him.

The reapportionment plan was finally approved by the court in early 1967. Republican Governor Claude Kirk had been elected, along with an almost entirely new legislature. The machinery of government was removed from the historical grasp of the so-called "Pork Choppers" of North Florida, and suddenly entrusted to a new, more bipartisan legislature dominated by South Florida legislators. Five of the old-timer leaders were gone, and the new legislature was comprised primarily of new members. A majority of the changes created several new seats that were located in the urban areas of Central and South Florida.

Later that day, after the breakfast meeting, Wayne left the house and went to the Jackson County courthouse, a check for the qualifying fee in his hand. He had decided.

"I knew Margie would not be happy, but I also knew she would once again stand by my side once she realized I was serious," Wayne says. "Once again, we had taken a new turn on our shared life-journey."

My First Campaign

"I knew I might have a difficult time beating the incumbent representative, Coy Mitchell, who was also from Jackson County, and was also well known in the district. This was evidenced when I began to canvass local county politicians. I repeatedly heard, 'I would like to support you, Wayne, but I can't because Coy Mitchell was instrumental in getting all state elected officials a significant raise during the last session, and I have to recognize what he accomplished for us.'"

Wayne continues, "I could understand their feelings of appreciation for Coy, and expressed that to them. Encountering this resistance made me fear that I had chosen a bad time to run. However, I later found that many of them just didn't vote in the special election because they also did not want to hurt my efforts. The work of a friend, Robert Asbell, was a big help during this first campaign. Robert was well known throughout the district. He was a local wholesale meat supplier. As a result, he made weekly deliveries throughout the region. He had an outgoing personality and was well liked by all who knew him. He took my campaign cards and distributed them as he made his routes. He also personally asked many of them to vote for me. From this experience I learned how important personal endorsements from friends were in influencing voters.

"I didn't spend a lot of money on newspaper and television advertising. Instead, I campaigned on the Main Street of the towns in the district. I soon learned how to shake the hand of a stranger as I introduced myself. I also participated in as many political rallies and forums as possible. I would always get there early and meet as many people as possible. Initially, Margie had a hard time engaging in the campaign. She is naturally shy and reserved and had to force herself to talk to strangers.

"Fortunately, we already knew a lot of people within the three counties which comprised my district, and that made campaigning much easier for both of us. Additionally, Margie had relatives scattered throughout the Panhandle (her great-great-great-grandfather had twenty-one children). We assumed all of her relatives voted for me.

"I got another big boost from Margie's mother, who had retired from her job as teacher at Graceville High School after many years of service. She became an active spokesperson for me. Her favorite punchline when she spoke was, 'You know Wayne Mixson has to be a wonderful person. He even has his mother-in-law supporting him!'"

Meanwhile, Margie's uncle, Jim Bowen, who lived in Washington County, used his local influence to help the campaign. He owned a popular hardware store in Chipley, and was in contact with a lot of the local citizens. Wayne loves to tell how his support grew. "In that first campaign he would ask them to vote for his sister's son in-law, Wayne Mixson. Later, when I ran for Lt. Governor, he had changed that request to, 'Please vote for my nephew, Wayne Mixson, who is running for Lt. Governor.' Then after I became Lt. Governor, he began answering the phone, 'Lt. Governor Wayne Mixson's uncle Jim speaking!' I always appreciated his support and enthusiasm."

Because it was a special election which had been hastily called, the length of the campaign was much shorter than normal. Since Wayne was new on the political scene and trying to beat a popular incumbent who was also a farmer, he feared the short campaign period might work to his disadvantage.

And the Winner Is . . .

At this time there was almost no Republican participation in any of the races in Northwest Florida. In two races that year, the Democratic candidate was unopposed. However, this was the beginning of a time of change in Florida's state politics. The influence of the new Republican governor, Claude Kirk,[2] and the impact of redistricting, moved the minority party forward across the state. The Republicans unexpectedly won enough positions and gained enough strength in both chambers to sustain the governor's vetoes.

When precinct totals began to be announced on election night, Wayne took an early lead. Wayne remembers, "We all held our breath as the results of the home precinct were announced. Coy Mitchell had won his home voting district, but not by a large margin, and I still held the lead. Shortly afterward the Marianna district results came in, and I won by a huge majority. At that point we knew the election was ours. I ended up winning by a two-to-one margin. I was suddenly the elected 7th District State Representative!"

Wayne Mixson's political career had been launched!

Endnotes

1. Known as the "Mark Out Coffee Club" because of a numbers game which is played each morning to determine which member has to pay for everyone's coffee, the club has over thirty members and has been on national television on several occasions for political polling of the community during elections.

2. Claude Kirk was the first Republican to be elected governor of Florida since the Reconstruction Era of 1877.

PART II

TWENTY YEARS OF PUBLIC SERVICE

1967–1987

Beginning with the legislative session of 1967, and for the next two decades, the state of Florida was undergoing a transition as significant as the changes created by the traumas of the Civil War and the Reconstruction Period (1860–1880). After the end of World War II, people began to flood into Florida, especially the southeastern coastal areas. This dynamic growth created problems with infrastructure, growth management, taxation, environment, education, expansion of government, conflict between agricultural interests and development needs, and countless other vitally important issues.

In the years before this period, North Florida had been where most of the population resided, where the control of state politics was held, and where a rural, conservative philosophy prevailed. In 1966 the Supreme Court ordered Florida's government to reapportion all districts in the state on a "one man, one vote" basis. Compliance with this order suddenly transferred political power in the state of Florida to the more liberal, urban areas of South Florida. The class of legislators that Wayne Mixson entered was full of many new faces, most from South Florida—among them a young Bob Graham.

Another change of tremendous importance that was underway

73

at this moment in history was the fact that incoming Republican governor Rubin Askew had ordered the legislature to write a new state constitution and reorganization of Florida's government. This unique opportunity was to be the very first task undertaken by Wayne Mixson and this session of the legislature. This era of Florida's history was to become recognized as the "Golden Age of Florida Politics." More critical legislation was enacted during this period than at any time since the state was founded.

Within a few years Wayne became chairman of the powerful Agricultural Committee, became a leader of the conservative element within the Democratic Party, and became the unofficial mediator when conflicts developed on legislation between the liberal, urban legislators and the rural, conservative legislators. Since Wayne had lived and been schooled in the urban North, he could often provide a unique understanding of the needs and viewpoints of both sides, and could often develop a compromise solution. Both groups began to turn to Wayne in designing and passing their proposed legislation.

After six terms covering twelve years, Wayne was preparing to retire and return to his farm, when announced gubernatorial candidate Bob Graham asked him to become his running mate for the position of lieutenant governor. After an eventful campaign, they won. Their two-term administration left a legacy of legislation and activities that have had tremendous impact on growth management, environmental protection, jobs development, education, and society in Florida for many decades.

Although Wayne Mixson was widely known and enjoyed popularity across the entire state, and was a likely choice for succeeding Bob Graham as the next governor of Florida, he opted to return to his farm in Jackson County and enjoy his remaining years in retirement with the love of his life, Margie.

CHAPTER SIX

THE LEGISLATIVE YEARS

1966–1978

The Political Environment in Florida in 1967

Wayne Mixson was beginning his political career in the Florida legislature at a unique moment in the history of government in Florida. It was a time of dramatic changes within the state, and these changes were thus creating dramatic changes in the government. The legislative changes that Wayne and his peers of this era were about to enact would impact the citizens of Florida for many decades into the future.

From the end of World War II in 1945, until the time of Wayne's election in 1967, Florida had changed from being a relatively sparsely populated state with an agriculturally based economy, into being a tourist and retirement mecca for the nation. Hundreds of thousands of new residents were flooding into the state and establishing residency, primarily in the southeastern coastal region from Orlando to Miami. At the same time, when Cuba's government was overthrown in 1958 and Fidel Castro took control and formed a Communist regime, a large influx of Cuban refugees flooded into South Florida. This populating and developing of the southern half of the Florida peninsula was changing the culture of the state, and simultaneously altering the balance of political power.

In the preceding hundred years, most of Florida's residents had lived in the northern half of the state. When Florida became the twenty-seventh state in 1845, the state's population was 40,000 residents who were lured there through a free land program. Most of these citizens lived on farms in the Panhandle and northern region, with Tallahassee the center of activity. Until the middle of the next century, the southern half of the state remained mostly undeveloped, sandy land with little population.

By the early 1960s that situation had changed, and the majority of the state's residents now lived in the southern half of the state, in newly developing urban sprawl. The economy in the southern region was booming from the impact of population growth and a flourishing tourism industry. Meanwhile, little had changed in the rural, agricultural, northern half of Florida. However, political control of the state remained in the north, due to creatively designed legislative voting district allocations by those in power. The unfairness of that system eventually led to lawsuits that reached the Supreme Court of the United States. The ruling of the high court required that the results of the November 1966 elections in Florida be thrown out, an approved redistricting plan be designed and implemented, and a second, special election be held to fill all vacancies. After several attempts and much negotiation, a redistricting plan was finally approved by the courts. It was passed by the legislature in early 1967, and a special election was set for February. This was the special election in which Wayne Mixson won and became the representative for the newly designed Seventh District in northwest Florida. When the freshman legislator, Representative Wayne Mixson, took his seat on the floor of the Florida House chamber early on that February morning on the opening day of the 1967 session, none in attendance realized the important role he was destined to play for the next twelve years.

This forced redistricting and special election dramatically changed the balance of power within Florida's legislative branch of government. The election suddenly took control from the group of north Florida conservative Democrats known as the Pork Chop Gang that had controlled Florida's government for decades. This special election had effectively removed their majority and transferred political control to the more liberal, multicultural, urban-focused Democrats of south Florida, where many new districts had been created and new representatives elected to office. There was an unusually large occurrence of new faces in the House chamber that first session when Wayne was sworn in.

Another very important political action that was underway as Wayne took his seat in the House chamber that day was a directive from the newly elected Republican governor, Claude Kirk, ordering the legislature to hold a special session dedicated to rewriting the Florida constitution. Once the legislature had prepared and approved the new state constitution, it would be submitted to the voters of the state for final approval in a special referendum.

After the new constitution was approved by the voters, the next step in the directive was for the legislature, through amendments, to completely redesign the organizational chart for state government in Florida, with the stated objective of eliminating duplications, removing unneeded functions, creating needed departments, and modernizing processes. These were to be Wayne's first assignments. What an exciting and unique opportunity for a first-term representative!

My First Day in the Legislature

Wayne vividly remembers when he and Margie arrived in Tallahassee for his first session. "The importance of the much-anticipated event of my first day in the State legislature was fully realized as Margie and I arrived at a Tallahassee motel the night before the opening session. A big bus with dozens of well-dressed and excited people was unloading and checking into the rooms adjoining us. On the side of the bus were long banners announcing congratulations to Jim Reeves, a newly elected member from Pensacola. We were all alone but enjoyed the spirit and excitement of the group.

"The following morning, dressed in our best clothes and full of excitement, we were both overwhelmed as we walked into the House chamber. The desk which had been designated for me was overflowing with many beautiful flower arrangements. Every desk was similarly decorated and it added to the beauty of the occasion.

"Margie took her seat in a special section of the gallery which had been set aside for our families. Everyone was dressed in full splendor and filled with eager anticipation of the swearing-in ceremony. The galleries were filled with family and well-wishers and the press box was filled with reporters from all the important news sources. The opening session of the Florida legislature was always a major event in Tallahassee.

"The session was called to order by the speaker. He delivered kind words, welcoming all of us and setting forth our task, stressing that it was time for action. I was in awe and somewhat comforted at all of the information and knowledge that our leaders must possess. In the presence of all of this preparation, we could only imagine how much more was yet to come.

"Then the ceremonial procession began. The cabinet members were recognized as they entered the chamber. The Senate members had been announced and taken their seats in chairs among us in the House Then the president of the Senate was recognized. In the days before the new constitution, he was the immediate successor to the governor. Then the climax of the entrance of Florida government officials arrived: 'Ladies and gentlemen, the governor of the great state of Florida,' as newly elected Governor Claude Kirk entered, and was recognized and seated. It would have seemed an impossibility that those words would someday announce my own entrance. At that moment, I was already over my capacity in excitement without any such foreseeing. Next, a justice of the Florida Supreme Court administered the oath of office to us in groups of six or eight. My group consisted of members from Jackson, Bay, and Leon County districts. By luck, Don Tucker[1] from Wakulla in Leon county, was in my group. Don later became House speaker and was the only House speaker to be reelected during my days. I later told Don that I wanted to become a close supporter, but that I was not one so party-bound that I could be depended on to support all party proposals.

"This proclaimed independence was a reservation I exacted from all future speakers. I think that the commitment to follow my own judgment and not party loyalty was a great strength for all of my political career. Fortunately, my primary assignment as chairman of the Agricultural Committee did not often lend itself to political interpretations.

"This all took place in the old, historic Florida Capital House chambers which were much smaller than today's new facilities. There was great excitement for all members and their families in having won the election, preparing for the first day, being finally sworn in, and ultimately taking our seats in the prestigious House of Representatives."

Getting Started

"I was very fortunate that I now represented District No. 7, which at the time had two members representing three counties. The other legislator from my district was an older member, Bill Inman, who was from Gadsden County. Bill was one of the few remaining veteran members who had served several terms in the House. He and I represented Jackson, Gadsden, and Liberty Counties, which formed our district.

"Seniority is very important in political protocol at all levels of elected office. For legislative members, it is also a primary factor in determining office assignments. Representative Inman had been assigned an office which was part of a two-office suite on the main hall. He and I together persuaded Ralph Turlington,[2] the new speaker, to give me the other office. We were only three doors down from the House chamber.

"Office space was scarce in the old capitol, so many of the 120 members were assigned offices in nearby state buildings, some two or three blocks away, while others were assigned very cramped space in the old, dusty loft of the Capitol building.

"My new office was the envy of many, and better than offices assigned to many veteran members. This location was convenient, but there were some disadvantages. Numerous lobbying interests were frequently gathered in the hall and rotunda between the House and Senate chambers. They were usually assigned by their client to make appointments with dozens of legislators as part of their daily business. My office was the first open door down from the House and was the most convenient place for every one of them to use who needed a telephone. Needless to say, we became friends with much of the lobbying community very rapidly. One of these friendly gentlemen was Chuck Hall, mayor of Miami Beach. I was always honored for him to drop by to chat and use our phone to make a call. It was indeed a coup for me to be able to accommodate such an important political figure in Florida.

"One day my secretary left me a note saying that 'Gus' Hall[3] had stopped by, not referring to him as 'Mayor.' I wondered why a nationally known socialist had called on me—I wasn't even a member of his organization. Later we laughed over this error in communication. I became good friends with Mayor Hall, and when he decided to run for governor the next year he asked me to run as lieutenant governor on the ticket with him. Feeling that I was not yet experienced enough to try to reach that far, I respectfully turned down his offer. This was a most flattering experience for a freshman legislator."

Wayne describes the political situation that existed in 1967. "The reapportionment and election in 1966-67 saw the disappearance of the historical one-party rule of the rural block known as the Pork Chop Gang. This election also brought to Florida a truly bipartisan legislature. In fact, in reality it was a 'tri-party' environment, because the Democratic group contained a significant segment of conservatives. The House of Representatives now had to learn to govern with three, not two, parties. The election had also brought forty new, conservative-leaning Republicans to the House.

"The sixty Democrats who were seated for that session were divided very sharply philosophically into the 'Old Democrats,' 'Conservative Florida Democrats' (or CFDs, as we called ourselves), and the new, more liberal Democratic members, most of whom represented districts in the southern areas of the state. Leadership in each of these parties was passionate in holding its ground philosophically. Indeed, the new third-party position was established and fortified by the frequent caucuses that were held to keep our group informed. The CFD members were the old, reelected conservative Democrats from about the state, combined with a new crop of conservative Democrats who could not follow the liberal line, nor had yet become Republicans.

"The CFD group had an attraction to many of the new members who were not yet attuned to the old partisan influences that had to be learned. CFD membership was identified by noting who showed up for the caucuses. We often wore a metal CFD badge on our lapel, and the regular Democrats, mostly from South Florida, were often surprised by who was wearing a CFD badge.

"Ralph Turlington of Gainesville was elected the first speaker of this new legislature. While living in Gainesville I had met Ralph, who was my legislator there. I had told him of my interest in running for the legislature from my home district in Jackson County. Ralph looked me over closely and then pronounced my evidence of being fit, as he said, 'You have a good head of hair. I think you will make it.' Coming from a very wise and experienced 'old-timer,' I took great encouragement. I would very soon discover that there were other requirements for serving that were more useful than a head of hair.

"But those were encouraging words for me, since they came from one of Florida's icons in state government. Ralph was so knowledgeable that he could debate for hours on any subject that came up and was almost always on the winning side. I voted for him every year as 'The Most Effective in Debate' member of the House. Much of the time neither I nor any other member knew what he was saying, but by supporting his views I was almost always right, and certainly on the winning side.

"The story was told that Ralph was outside the House chamber on one occasion when one of the speaker's favored bills was in trouble in debate. He sent a messenger for Ralph to come quickly and help. Ralph rushed in the door, grabbed his microphone, and spoke eloquently for ten minutes before he knew what the bill was about.

"I vividly remember an occasion when House Speaker Ralph Turlington reprimanded Representative Bill Choppel of Ocala, who was a CFO, by stating that Choppel and his delegation should 'Behave like Democrats.' Bill immediately retorted by publicly replying, 'The Republicans have already moved northward in Florida as far as Marion County, and if we vote the way Speaker Turlington is asking us to vote, they will elect Republicans and replace both of us in our own counties next election.' Indeed, partisan politics had become very much alive in Florida. Fortunately, our occupation that first year was to write a new constitution for the state of Florida, and most of the issues involved in that task did not lend themselves to partisan considerations.

"The number of Republican legislators was growing and debates on the floor were often defined by partisan positions. I considered myself to be conservative, but always tried to develop my position on an issue by consideration of merit, instead of partisanship. That was always one of my guiding principles.

"I was indeed pleased to have my friend Ralph as my speaker. He gave me excellent committee assignments. As a freshman, I was assigned to the Appropriations Committee, the Rules Committee, and the Agricultural Committee. These important committee assignments served me well throughout my legislative service. Next term I was elected chairman of the Agricultural and General

Legislative Committees, and served for several years as chairman of the General Government Subcommittee on the Appropriations Committee."

Writing A New Constitution

Not only did Florida have a bipartisan legislative membership for the first time with the 1967 session, but it also had a new Republican governor. Governor Claude Kirk wasted no time after his election to call for a special session to rewrite the old constitution. Thus this new legislative body, most of which had never served in any capacity, and a new governor who had no experience in government nor any other elective office, were both suddenly challenged with a monumental project.

Wayne was very fortunate and privileged to have this constitutional rewrite as one of the very first tasks that he was assigned as a legislator. Imagine the historical importance of participating in the complete rewriting of the Florida constitution—something that no legislators had enjoyed the privilege of doing since 1885.

Participating in this exciting task immediately exposed Wayne to virtually every state agency and its mission, identification of areas of waste where the passage of time had created unnecessary functions, duplications, potentials for consolidations, existing bottlenecks, and areas where modernization was needed. It was a unique and extremely effective indoctrination exercise for a new legislator.

Wayne describes this exciting work, "During the next three months we were all to become much better informed as we worked to create a much shorter and improved version of the constitution. We dealt with leaving out much of the massive language that had been added over time, most of which should have originally been statutory provisions instead of constitutional. The 1885 Constitution had intentionally been designed to limit the power of the executive branch and the powers of the governor, after the

Reconstruction years. The original document divided and diluted the chief executive's powers by creating six other elected top executives who shared power with the governor. These were the attorney general, the education commissioner, the state treasurer, the commissioner of agriculture, commissioner of insurance, and state comptroller.

"At the time we began our work there was general support to have the governor's position created in the state constitution, and the other offices created by statute. This was an effort to strengthen the governor's powers and limit the powers of the cabinet members. Florida was the only state in the union which had made all cabinet members constitutional positions. Through succeeding years constitutional amendments have changed this provision, leaving only the attorney general and the commissioner of agriculture as elected, along with the governor.

"In my opinion, this is probably a good balance for the state. The governor now exercises most executive powers but shares some functions with the other cabinet members."

The Constitution Session

Rewriting or creating a new constitution for a state like Florida was a major undertaking. Most of this new legislature had no legal training, little knowledge of the constitution and its real purpose, and no legislative experience. At the same time, they all realized that it was a unique opportunity to quickly accomplish a giant step forward for the state. As a group, they dove into the task, determined to do the best possible work. Wayne describes how they approached their assignment.

"None felt this handicap of inexperience more acutely than I did. Florida's citizens, who had just elected us to this task, must have questioned the wisdom of the governor's call for the rewrite as the first item on the agenda for such a group. As we prepared for the rewriting, we held early meetings with constitutional experts, legal scholars, members of the Florida Supreme Court and trial courts. A panel of such experts had already studied the constitution and presented their recommended provisions for the new constitution.

"Many feel a constitution is a cold, abstract, forbidding, mysterious document, only for lawyers and judges to understand. Not so. What is a constitution, and where does it derive its powers? These questions had to be answered for each of us before we could begin to work. Ancient Rome hit on the idea of reciprocal rights and duties under law, giving concreteness by treating them as contracts. In this way, freedom emanating from a constitutional order had been advocated by establishing the presumption that civilized society is founded on a public social contract. It is a voluntary agreement, and is likely to be observed, or can be enforced by law. Everybody gets something. My faith is that the more we know of the origin and intent of our founding fathers, the greater pride we have in our country.

"James Madison said, 'The constitutional system prevails when every man in or out of office is bound by lawful contracts. Without constitutional government there is no freedom.' One of the earliest documents granting freedom to citizens of a nation was the Magna Carta[4] of England in 1225. It provided that no free man would be imprisoned without due process of law. It thus limited the king and the tax-collecting authority.

"This concept was further developed when John Locke,[5] Blackstone,[6] and others wrote, 'The King's power comes not from God but from the consent of the people who are endowed with unalienable rights of life, liberty, and property.' This was a remarkable new approach to government that was later to become a cornerstone for our American constitution. Armed with these inspirational facts, and feeling the empowering authority of free people, we set out on a four-month task of rewriting the Florida constitution. It proved to be a most enlightening and enjoyable task for me. We provided that the constitution is reviewed by an appointed commission each ten years.

"The people can make revisions as they choose, thus keeping the constitution relevant to current times. The constitution that we developed was approved by the citizens of Florida in 1968. It replaced the old 1885 constitution with about half as many words. A state constitution provides a limitation on the powers of the elected and executive officials of the state. The constitution is a grant of powers to the government from the people of the state.

"We were especially proud of the final product, Florida's new constitution of 1968. It consisted of only 30,000 words. One important provision in the new constitution was the requirement that, in a special session of the legislature, a new organization for Florida's government should subsequently be designed and submitted for approval through the amendment procedure. We all realized that huge gains in cost reductions and improved efficiencies could be realized through reorganization."

Early in the process of writing the constitution, one contested issue that arose was the need for converting the budgeting and required sessions from a biannual system to an annual system. In 1885 the population of Florida, the size and complexity of the budget, and the need for constant government availability were much different from the situation that existed in 1967–1969, when the new constitution and amendments were being created by Wayne and his fellow legislators. The job of a state legislator had changed from a part-time, gentleman patriot function into the need for a full-time, skilled politician working constantly to serve the needs of his or her district.

During discussions, some of the old-time legislators wanted to maintain the alternating-year sessions and two-year budgeting approach, citing that an annual approach would convert the activities of the legislature into being continuously consumed in budgeting. However, with the tremendous growth that was underway in the state, and the resulting problems in managing development, protection of the environment, infrastructure needs, and funding, the need for full-time legislative attention was obvious. Thus, the constitution of 1968 created annual budgeting and annual sessions for Florida's government. Wayne continues, describing major changes in the new constitution.

"The revamped document reorganized the executive branch, allowed a governor to only serve two terms, created an elected post of lieutenant governor, created five appointed cabinet offices, enhanced the Department of Commerce, and included a 'declaration of rights,' which guaranteed citizens freedom from racial or religious discrimination.

"The new charter also established 'home rule'[7] for Florida counties, and established a limit of 10 mils on local taxation. The new document also required that Florida's government meet annually and approve an annual budget, rather than the biannual approach that had been appropriate in 1885. It required the state to always function under a balanced budget. It also clearly states that the constitution derives its authority from a grant of powers from the people of the state of Florida.

"The new constitution was approved in referendum by the citizens of Florida by a wide margin in 1968. It then legally replaced the old constitution of 1885. I was very pleased with what we had accomplished, and especially proud to have participated in the process.

"Next, we worked into the regular order of things after the new constitution was approved by referendum, as we began the constitutionally required governmental reorganization session in 1969. The resulting amendments defining the reorganization were subsequently approved by the legislature and voted into law. The changes created in this body of amendments were dramatic. The old constitution, that had grown to require 150-plus government agencies, was reorganized into only twenty new departments. The resulting savings from removal of obsolete requirements and removal of duplications, along with improvements in speed and efficiency, were remarkable."

Legislative Accomplishments 1967–1979

The first two years of service by Wayne Mixson as a state representative were consumed by what were probably the most important and lasting accomplishments that he, or any other Florida legislator, would undertake in the next hundred years. These years, 1967 and 1968, were almost totally dedicated to authoring a new, modernized Florida constitution, obtaining legislative and referendum approvals, then preparing a body of initial amendments in order to redesign the organizational structure of Florida's government, and again achieving required approvals for enactment. The citizens of Florida are still realizing the benefits of the legislative work completed during those two critical years.

Thus in this impressive manner was launched what was to become a twelve-year, six-term, tenure for Representative Wayne Mixson. During this critical era in Florida's demographic, governmental, economic, environmental, and social evolution, Wayne was destined to play an important role. This section of his biography will describe some of the most notable legislative actions of those years, and Wayne will tell the real story of what happened.

Thousands of new residents were pouring into Florida each week, as unprecedented growth occurred. Water problems,·environmental considerations, taxation issues, and growth management items brought on by Florida's rapid growth came to the forefront of legislative attention during these years. There was sufficient partisan agreement on these major issues to enable the passage of several foundational pieces of legislation in this period. The Florida Legislature was later cited nationally for its prompt attention and satisfactory solutions to the commanding issues of this era.

Agricultural Land Taxation

Wayne describes some of the problems that were facing farmers in Florida. "Agriculture has always been one of the largest segments of the Florida economy. Farming had been a way of subsistence for the first settlers, with little or no commercial impact. Initial commercialization of farming in Florida was difficult, since soils were not naturally fertile, and its semitropical wet and warm climate was a perfect host to all insects and airborne plant diseases in existence. There was either too much or too little water for most agricultural products. Drainage and/or irrigation was necessary for many crops. An abundance of plant and animal pests required application of pesticides on most crops, and much had to be applied by airplanes.

As agricultural technologies advanced, most of these initial problems were resolved, and agribusiness remained a major element of Florida's economy. Sugar cane and vegetable farms flourished in South Florida and a huge citrus industry developed in Central Florida, while peanuts, cotton, and soybeans dominated in North Florida. As our state's population began to grow at astounding rates, it was necessary that property classified as agricultural land be developed commercially to provide the housing and infrastructure these new residents needed. In many areas, this frequent encroachment and change of use created problems. Among the most serious of these was taxation of farmland, as the land values increased because of approaching development. I knew that our legislature had to provide management of this growth, and resolution of the problems that it was creating throughout the state."

Since Wayne Mixson's background was deeply rooted in Florida agriculture, he soon became a major contributor to the development of state agricultural policies. As chairman of the powerful Agricultural Committee, he was positioned to protect farming interests as commercial development increased throughout the state. He describes the problems related to property taxation.

"Florida was a rapidly growing urban state, but we had to make room for agriculture to also exist. Taxation and regulations had to be reconciled to meet the needs of growing urban realities. Rapid urban growth and its required property development encroached on some of Florida's best farmland.

"As this occurred a serious problem developed in property taxation procedures. County tax assessors were required to assess all land at full value. Speculation suddenly elevated these farm and ranch valuations, and thus created tax burdens for many farmers that were far beyond their ability to pay. The farmer frequently had to sell his farm to the developers or go out of business. Often tax assessors recognized these limitations and made some local adjustments to help farmers survive. I realized that it was necessary for the new constitution to provide a remedy for these problems.

"Agriculture ranks high as a job producer and as an economic engine in almost every county in Florida. I prepared an amendment, along with others, to allow a remedy for the taxation problem. 'Agricultural lands in Florida may be assessed and taxed on the basis of their use.' This language was approved in the new constitution.

"This provision allows the farmer to engage in the various agricultural land use and be taxed on the economic value of its use. On the same section of land there could be one value for growing trees, another for growing citrus, and another for cattle grazing. These same values could apply to adjoining property of the same character. In other words, the farmer may choose his agricultural enterprise and expect fair taxation. I often refer to these accommodations as recognition that 'Agriculture must be cultivated in Florida to survive.' I am very proud to have helped develop this fair approach to taxing farm land as urban growth is occurring."

Legislative Pay Raise Bill

Soon after the reorganization amendments had been approved, a bill was presented that provided a 50 percent increase in pay for Florida's legislators. The bill was brought forward by pressure from the more liberal South Florida Democratic contingent. Wayne publicly spoke out with strong opposition against this bill. He describes his feelings: "The Florida legislature, in the new state district format, became more influenced by urban areas. This more liberal element soon provided significant pay raises for county offices, then legislative staff, and finally moved to raise legislative salaries to $12,000 per year, a very high figure for the time. For many years, my local Jackson County office was in the county courthouse in Marianna, with Mrs. Jean Daniel as my administrative assistant. I argued against the proposed raise, and voted against the bill which created the increase. I felt strongly that it was wrong for us to pass a raise during the middle of a term. In fact, the legality of the raise was contested in the state courts for several months. After the bill was passed, Governor Kirk vetoed the measure, and the determined group in the legislature organized and overruled his veto.

"My pay raise amounted to about $4,000 for the year. I first attempted to refuse it. When that failed, I next tried to give it back to the State. Finally, I donated it to the charity funds in the state institutions that were located within my district. These included the patients' fund at the Chattahoochee State Hospital, Dozier School for Boys, and two penal institutions. I would have felt guilty if I had conceded and taken the raise that year. It was a matter of principle for me. In debate, I had stated that I would refuse to take it.

"In 1968 I was reelected for a second term with almost 60 percent of the vote. In 1970 I had no opposition, then in 1972 I again won by a wide margin. By then I was well known in the district and had many loyal supporters. I am deeply grateful for all they did for me."

The Open Records Law

The first public records law in Florida was passed in 1908. A much-needed replacement law was prepared and submitted to the new legislature in the 1967 session. This law required that most government meetings be conducted in public, and it greatly expanded the public's access to government records. This law established the concept of "Government in the Sunshine," which has since enabled Florida's voters to maintain a watchful eye on the behavior of their elected officials and the bureaucracy. All government records were proclaimed to be public unless deemed to be "confidential" by an appropriate authority. Later, in 1992, the voters amended the state constitution to include a similar provision.

Wayne comments on the passage of this law: "I wholeheartedly supported passage of this bill, and I voted for it. I feel this legislation was another important improvement in Florida's government processes. It has undoubtedly reduced deceptive government activities in our state at all levels. I am glad I took part in passing that legislation."

Urban Renewal in South Florida

Early in Wayne's second term, the South Florida members brought forth a piece of urban vs. rural legislation which would involve use of state and federal funds for a program to provide urban redevelopment in an area of Miami. This bill was resisted by many members from North Florida who did not want to see state funds of this magnitude spent on a Miami social project. Wayne shocked many of his rural, ultraconservative friends in the CFD group when he agreed to co-sponsor the Federal Urban Renewal Legislation with the Dade County representative, Gerald Lewis. Wayne explains the reasons why he sided with the South Florida members on this issue.

"There were several factors which caused me to decide to promote this piece of social legislation. First, I was a member of the Urban Affairs Committee and had been on tours to look at urban development projects in New York, Atlanta, and other cities. I had seen places where this approach was working and improving people's lives.

"Second, I had always felt a desire to help those who were living in substandard housing. This concern initiates in my childhood days and seeing the rural housing of farm laborers. Third, after reapportionment had strengthened the voting power of the urban contingent in the House, they had not been overly aggressive and had worked to reduce conflicts with rural interests. I felt my move would represent a demonstration of good faith. Fourth, I had always spoken out against measures which increased the involvement of the federal government in state affairs. This bill designated the state as having full control and management of the project. Fifth, since I had lived in northern cities while I was in college, I had a better understanding of the need for housing in urban areas, and last, I held hope that if the Miami project was successful, it might open the opportunity for similar projects in areas of need around the state, including my district. The decaying remnants of housing from the 'Old South' were the most visible needs for aiding the poor in these rural areas. I was in favor of any measure that would provide upgraded, modern living environments for our citizens. I always judged proposed legislation on merit, and I felt this program had merit.

"The only portion of the urban development bill that I disliked was the fact that it did involve using the power of eminent domain to obtain some of the needed properties for the project. I detested the concept of seizing private property from one owner and then developing the land for another private use. However, in this case I decided the good would outweigh the bad, and local people would make the decision in referendum."

There was an important benefit that developed as a result of Wayne's stance on this urban measure. His support established the fact that he was not going to always be a party-aligned, dogmatic conservative in every instance. His assistance in getting this measure passed was to greatly enhance his acceptance by those who could have been political roadblocks on future matters. It began the recognition by both opposing sides that Wayne was uniquely positioned to be an "emissary of compromise" when disputes arose.

The Reubin Askew Era (1970–1978)

In 1970 Republican governor Claude Kirk was defeated by Reubin Askew,[8] a Democratic state senator from Pensacola. He was to go on to win another term in 1974. Wayne gives his impression of Askew: "I soon found him to be an agreeable, down-to-earth type of man, who had a strong desire to remove corruption and favoritism from state government. He personally led a petition drive to require all public officials to disclose their personal finances, in order to prevent hidden incidences of a conflict of interest. I agreed with him and supported his initiatives."

Candidacy For Merit Act

In 1970 Wayne earned the respect and support of many state employees when he introduced the Candidacy for Merit Bill. This bill removed the restriction which had previously existed which prohibited state employees who were under the merit system from running for public office. Because of this rule many talented people were not able to fully realize their potential, and the government was deprived of the benefits which their skills could provide.

Wayne describes what happened: "I felt the restrictions that kept wonderfully qualified government employees from ever seeking office was a very bad idea. I proposed removing this rule so that we could all benefit from this storehouse of experience and skill. The bill gained support and passed easily. As a result, in the years since passage many former state workers have run for offices around the state and they have made great contributions to the progress of their communities and the state of Florida. I am happy that I was able to help make this possible."

Becoming "Mr. Chairman"

In 1971 Richard "Dick" Pettigrew[9] was selected as speaker of the House. As he was forming the makeup of the House committees, Wayne was offered the prestigious and powerful position of chairman of the House Agricultural Committee. At the time he was the only real farmer remaining on the committee. In fact, there were few farmers in the entire legislature.

Due to the power this position afforded, Wayne's support, or lack of support, for any pending legislation became much more important to his peers. Wayne describes his feelings, "My fellow legislators knew that I would always represent the best interest of agriculture in Florida, so I seldom had any opposition on farm legislation.

"At this time Earl Hutto[10] of Panama City was a representative. Earl was also raised in the South Alabama region, and we were great friends. Earl, Pat Thomas[11] of Quincy, and I all sat near each other in the House chamber, so we often had the opportunity to talk privately.

"The following session, Terrell Sessums[12] was selected as the new speaker. I was again designated as the chairman of the Agricultural Committee. During his term, I worked closely with Speaker Sessums to accomplish expansion of the Tampa Fairgrounds."

The Baker Act

During 1971 Wayne promoted the passage of the Florida Mental Health Act, which later became known as the Baker Act. Wayne explains why he supported this legislation. "Prior to this legislation many elderly and handicapped citizens in Florida were being abused by family members, who would find a doctor to attest that an individual was insane and then have them committed to the Florida State Hospital in Chattahoochee. This system was being abused by families who merely wanted relief from the burden of caring for handicapped or aging family members.

"The system was also being abused by criminals who could escape prosecution for a crime by finding a doctor who would declare them insane, being committed for a period of time, and then being declared sane by the hospital doctors. They could then be released back into society by a court without ever being sent to prison.

"The new legislation strengthened the requirements for commitment and provided for involuntary examinations ordered by judges, physicians, law enforcement officials, or mental health professionals. It also required that in cases of release, the court granting the release be the same court that had ordered the commitment. This assures a greater level of familiarity with the case when the release decision is made."

The University of Florida School of Veterinary Medicine

During this era, while Wayne Mixson was serving as chairman of the Agricultural Committee, he initiated a movement within the legislature to fund the construction of a facility to house a school of Veterinary Science on the campus of the University of Florida in Gainesville, as well as funding other start-up needs. Due to his long-time involvement with Florida agribusiness, this proposal was very important to him. Wayne describes his feelings, "The bill had wide support, and passed relatively easily in the legislature. We knew that a great need existed within the state for veterinarians and felt it was important that our university system provide those professionals.

"I am especially proud of the role I played in helping with the passage of funding for the establishment of the Veterinary Medicine College at the University of Florida. I consider it one of my crowning achievements. We had documented that in many farm areas the farmers were having a difficult time caring for their farm animals because of a shortage of veterinary services within the state. We estimated that there was a need for around 1,000 additional veterinarians. The bill which I actively sponsored for funding the new facility and school at the University was passed, and now the school produces a much-needed class of veterinarians every year."

Margie's Victory

It was difficult for Wayne to discuss this part of his life with Margie. "In 1971 life was good for us. We were blessed with a wonderful marriage, a loving and supportive family, we owned a thriving, productive farm, I had been elected to an important political position, and Margie had a fulfilling teaching career. At this time, she had moved from teaching at the high school level to being an instructor at Chipola College in Marianna. Then our lovely world was suddenly shaken. Margie was diagnosed with breast cancer!

"In those days most women were hesitant to discuss breast cancer. One reason for this hesitancy was due to the high mortality rate that the cancer created, and another reason was that many people felt it was inappropriate to discuss a woman's breast.

"After the diagnosis in Marianna, Margie was referred to a doctor at Emory University Hospital in Atlanta for surgery. Margie says it was one of the darkest days of her life when she awoke after the mastectomy, and feeling that she was probably going to die. She felt that even if she did survive, her life would be miserable because of limited activities and embarrassment over a perceived change in appearance. I tried to express my enduring love for her, and that the most important thing was her survival. I stressed that the other concerns were of little significance even though they meant a lot to her at the time. I tried to get her to focus on the many wonderful years that lay ahead for us to share.

"Then something wonderful happened that lifted her out of the post-operative depression. A stranger came into her hospital room.

She was a very attractive, well-dressed woman who introduced herself as a member of Reach to Recovery,[13] a program affiliated with the American Cancer Society. As she introduced herself and shook Margie's hand, she said, "I have had the same surgery that you just had." Then she began to tell us how active her life was, playing golf and tennis, and she certainly did not look deformed or depressed.

"After she talked with Margie for a while, I could see the depression lifting and a much more positive outlook taking its place. After she left, Margie looked at me and said in a determined voice, 'If she can do it, I can do it!'

"The following year, 1972, Margie endured another mastectomy after another malignancy was discovered, but this time she did not let the surgery impact her negatively. I was very proud of her strength and determination. She is a very brave and capable woman."

Ever since she had this experience, Margie has been an active volunteer for the American Cancer Society, becoming president of the Leon County unit and a member of the state board. She also became a Reach to Recovery volunteer, helping many other women through the terrible experience of breast cancer. Every time a woman would have this treatment at Tallahassee Memorial Hospital, Margie would be called.

"The day after the surgery Margie would visit the woman during recovery. She would begin the visit by saying those same words she heard at Emory Hospital, 'I've had the same surgery that you just had.' She explains that she has been cancer-free for over forty years.

"Margie always came away from these visits inspired by the knowledge that she was helping these women during a time of need. She often said that she could see the change in attitude and growing hope in their faces as they talked. She always told them that after they recovered from the surgery, they would appreciate life even more, because every day is special.

"I was especially proud of Margie when in 1984 she was named the 'Tallahassee Democrat Volunteer of the Year in Social Services.' We have a beautiful memorial figurine trophy which she received at the award ceremony. Margie has always led an active life She has been at my side throughout my career, helping in any way she can. I have always been proud to have her standing with me.

"Margie has always enjoyed traveling with me on political trips when possible, plus we have traveled extensively on personal trips. She also is an avid (and capable) bridge player, and she loves to read. Perhaps her greatest attribute is her ability to make other people feel good. She is renowned for being a gracious host and has thus been a tremendous asset to my career. Although enduring breast cancer is a terrible experience, the old adage that 'with everything bad there is some accompanying goodness' was true for us. Sharing the suffering and life-threatening experience of cancer, along with the changes it made in our approach to life, strengthened our love and relationship. I thank God for the way it all turned out."

Agricultural Bills and Issues

Wayne reflectively discusses many of the legislative issues in which he played an instrumental role. "The following session, Speaker Pettigrew passed his gavel to incoming speaker, Terrell Sessums. I was again appointed as the chairman of the Agricultural Committee. During this term I worked closely with Speaker Sessums to accomplish expansion of the Tampa fairgrounds. While I was chairman of the Agricultural Committee we handled dozens of substantive pieces of legislation, but since they were agriculture-related, there was little partisan debate on them. I worked aggressively to support the rapidly expanding relevance of agriculture in the state while rapid urbanization was also occurring.

"Some of the important legislation which came to the forefront during this era included the Green Belt Law, legislation dealing with use of agricultural pesticides and livestock inventory legislation. The Green Belt Law shielded the state's farmers from a level of taxation that would have ruined the industry. Florida's agricultural pesticides legislation preceded the Environmental Protection Act of 1972. Since agriculture is a large consumer of water, the water conservation legislation passed during this time was of special interest to our committee. Through all of these issues, and the corresponding legislation which was passed, I played an important role and was able to protect Florida's farmers.

"I recall one instance when two of my fellow legislators had devised a scheme for getting $1.8 million dollars removed from the agricultural budget for use in a pet educational project they were promoting. The funds had been placed in the agricultural budget to eradicate cattle brucellosis, which was threatening feed and dairy herds in the state. They had devised a plan which used house parliamentary rules to block reconsideration of their bill which transferred the funds. However, I managed to get to the floor at a critical moment in their procedure and instead entered the motion to reconsider. After additional maneuvering and debating on my part, the funds remained in the agricultural budget.

"Another area of concern, and occasional political conflict, was legislation related to the working conditions, status, and compensation of migrant farm workers. As chairman of the Agriculture and Citrus Committee I was immersed in all of these issues as they came to the legislature. The migrant workers' union persistently pushed for added benefits for these workers while I attempted to restrain the potential disaster these added costs represented for the farmers in the state. Measures were promoted to force farmers to pay these workers the prevailing minimum wage and to provide them with worker's compensation insurance. I was in favor of legislation which assured the workers adequate living conditions, prohibition of child labor, and a reasonable level of compensation. I knew that providing workman's compensation insurance would be too expensive for the industry to consider. I feel that a reasonable compromise was achieved.

"Another very important accomplishment at this time was the establishment of the Veterinary Medicine College at the University of Florida. I am proud to be the legislator who initiated the movement to fund the new school at the university. The Agricultural Committee handled many other pieces of legislation which were not farm related. These were processed under the heading of 'General Bills.' I take great satisfaction in knowing how much we helped Florida's farmers during this difficult period in Florida's history."

Issues of the Day

"I was also recognized as a moderate on many non-farm issues. I was a supporter of the controversial 'Death with Dignity Bill,' which did not pass. I also was a progressive on most environmental issues, even though some were unpopular with many sectors. I generally supported the efforts of Governor Askew on these issues. At one point Askew encountered opposition from his own cabinet over a consumer advocacy issue, and I supported his position in that dispute. These are examples of why I was generally respected for following my own beliefs instead of being swayed by lobbyists or self-serving interests."

Property Tax Limits

"Another issue which has always been one of my priorities was controlling the use of property taxes for purposes which should be funded through a broader basis of taxation. The hapless property owners should not be forced to be the funding source for services which the total population enjoys. For that reason, in 1974 I promoted a constitutional amendment which would cap the school tax millage in counties at 7%. I felt the remainder of school funding should be derived from the general fund, or from non-earmarked funds in the budget. Initially the concept received a cool reception, but after debate and counsel more and more of my fellow legislators began to endorse the concept. Finally, even Governor Askew proposed including this amendment proposal on the ballot. The cap remains in place today."

Right-to-Work

"In a bipartisan effort, I led a movement in the House to implement the right-to-work constitutional provision. A similar movement was simultaneously launched in the Senate. With the help of the Florida Right to Work Committee, we promoted the passage of the bill across the state and within the legislative branch.

"The issue was very relevant to me since I could well remember when I had been forced to terminate my employment as a summer student worker at the Panama City paper mill because I would not join their union. I felt that a worker should have the right to choose whether or not they wanted to participate in union activities.

"Unionization and the right-to-work issue was also an important issue for Florida's agricultural sector, and as chairman of the Agricultural Committee, I had a responsibility to be involved in the passage of this important legislation. The bill provided that no employer can force an employee to join a union as a condition of employment, that no agricultural worker can be required to have any connection with a labor union as a condition of employment, and that any authorization for deduction of union dues from an employee's earnings must be in written form, and must be revocable at the will of the employee at any time. The bill also provided for fines and possible jail time for violations."

Use of Impact Fees—My Fish Pond Tale

In 1975 a bill was presented which would enable counties and cities to levy "impact fees" on new construction. Proponents of these fees felt the charges were justified because of the potential impact that such projects could have on local infrastructure, such as roads, schools, and law enforcement. Opponents of these fees felt that this approach was an "anti-business" policy which would hurt Florida's revitalized industrial development effort. The bill was promoted primarily by urban districts in South Florida, where they were having trouble managing and funding their tremendous growth. This legislation would enable local government to require developers to share the associated cost to the community for new development. Wayne recalls when this bill was proposed.

"I was recognized as an avid promoter of industry, to have a deep desire to bring more industrial jobs to Florida, and had sponsored several bills designed to lower or restrain property taxation. On the issue of impact fees, I once again surprised many of my peers when I publicly supported them.

"I spoke during the debate on the issue of impact fees on the House floor. I was in favor of passing the bill which enabled local governments to enact this tax if they so wished. I told this story: 'Not long ago I built a little fishpond on my farm. It cost me $1,100 to run an electrical line to it in order to operate a pump, which was needed to keep the pond filled. Now, there are two ways that could be used to pay for that electrical line. Wayne Mixson could have paid for it, or 100 people who all used the system could have paid for it. I don't want my neighbors to have to pay my light bill, so I paid for it. If we do not pass this bill, we will be adding taxes on everybody else just to pay the extra cost for services which is created by new construction. Actually, for existing taxpayers, this is a tax relief bill.

"A lot of people felt that my little speech and example I provided was a deciding factor in the passage of the bill. I felt it was the fairest approach. In District 11, which I represented, 'growth' was not a dirty word. We needed all of the new industry and new jobs we could get. Impact fees would be ill-considered in some areas. But I realized that in Florida, growth was occurring so rapidly that it was going to cause an unfair rise in property taxes for existing citizens. In order to provide orderly growth, fair taxation, and adequate infrastructure, such a program is necessary in Florida."

My Sixth Term and Retirement

Wayne discusses his feelings as he entered his sixth term as a legislator. "There are generally four reasons representatives leave their positions. First, some are not reelected. Second, declining health or aging. Third, disillusionment with the processes. Fourth, resigning to run for something else or to take an appointed position. When I returned to the House to begin my sixth term, I found it filled with new faces. Most of my old friends and associates were gone. The classes of 1967 through 1972 were considered by many to be among the finest in the body's history, and many had moved to the state Senate or to statewide positions. Twelve years had passed since I began my political role, and I was approaching the milestone of being sixty years old. Even the swearing-in ceremony, which had once thrilled Margie and me so much, was becoming less exciting.

"I discussed the issue with Margie, and we decided that I would retire at the end of my sixth term. We realized we were about to take another important turn on our life-journey. There was no reason, other than realizing that it was time for me to move on, which made me announce that I would not run for reelection in 1978. In a June 1978 issue of the *Jackson County Floridan*, the front page featured a pencil sketch picture of me with bold, blue lettering of a headline which said, 'District 7 Representative Retires After 12 Years.' The ensuing article flattered me as it reviewed my career and legislative accomplishments.

"At this point of my career, I envisioned returning to the farm with Margie and riding my tractor off into the sunset, but God had other important work for me to accomplish in my remaining productive years."

Discussion

As a state representative, Wayne Mixson played a very important leadership role for Florida during what was one of the most legislatively productive eras in Florida history—an era which has been awarded the title, "The Golden Age of Florida Legislation." Beginning with the creation of a new, modernized state constitution and a radical reorganization of Florida's government, followed by twelve years of legislative service which included much of the foundational legislation for governing, the work accomplished during this era has endured and continues to serve the citizens of Florida. Wayne Mixson was one of the founding fathers of the modern Florida we enjoy today. Additionally, some feel that because of his activities with Farm Bureau in Florida, and the significant impact of all of his sponsored farm legislation during his twelve years on the House Agricultural Committee, he should be recognized as the "Father of Florida Agriculture."

Endnotes

1. Donald L. Tucker (born July 23, 1935) is a former speaker of the Florida House of Representatives and special ambassador for the United States to the Dominican Republic. Tucker earned his Juris Doctorate degree from the University of Florida in 1962. He served as speaker of the Florida House of Representatives from 1974 to 1978. The Tallahassee-Leon County Civic Center was renamed in honor of Tucker in 1977 and is now known as the Donald L. Tucker Center.

2. Ralph Donald Turlington Sr. (born October 5, 1920) is a retired politician from the state of Florida. Turlington was born in Gainesville and attended the University of Florida to obtain a Bachelor of Science degree in business and then Harvard University for his Master's degree in the same field. He was elected to the Florida House of Representatives in 1950 for Alachua County. He would serve until 1974, eventually also serving as speaker from 1967 to 1969. He was the Florida Commissioner of Education from 1974 to 1987.

3. Gus Hall was a leader and chairman of the Communist Party USA and its four-time U.S. presidential candidate. As a labor leader, Hall was closely associated with the so-called Little Steel Strike of 1937, an effort to unionize the nation's smaller, regional steel manufacturers.

4. Magna Carta, English Great Charter, charter of English liberties granted by King John under threat of civil war, and reissued with alterations in 1216, 1217, and 1225. By declaring the sovereign to be subject to the rule of law, and documenting the liberties held by "free men," the Magna Carta would provide the foundation of individual rights in Anglo-American jurisprudence.

5. John Locke (August 29, 1632–October 28, 1704) was an English philosopher and physician, widely regarded as one of the most influential of Enlightenment thinkers and commonly known as the "Father of Liberalism." His writings influenced Voltaire, Rousseau, and many Scottish Enlightenment thinkers, as well as the American Revolutionaries. His contributions to classical republicanism and liberal theory are reflected in the United States Declaration of Independence.

6. Sir William Blackstone (July 10, 1723–February 14, 1780) was an English jurist and Tory politician of the eighteenth century. He is

most noted for writing the *Commentaries on the Laws of England,* an influential 18th-century treatise on the common law of England, originally published by the Clarendon Press at Oxford, 1765-1769. The work is divided into four volumes: on the rights of persons, the rights of things, of private wrongs, and of public wrongs. The *Commentaries* was long regarded as the leading work on the development of English law and played a role in the development of the American legal system.

7. Home Rule. The rights given to local self-government, including the powers to regulate for the protection of the public health, safety, morals, and welfare; to license; to tax; and to incur debt. Relates to the power of a local city or county to set up its own system of governing and local ordinances without receiving a charter from the state which comes with certain requirements and limitations. The concept has become popular with so-called libertarians, survivalists, and others who would like to divorce local government from as much state regulation as possible. This does not mean they cannot take state funds for local needs.

8. Reubin O'Donovan Askew was an American politician who served as the 37th governor of Florida from 1971 to 1979. He led on tax reform, civil rights, and financial transparency for public officials, maintaining an outstanding reputation for personal integrity. Askew is widely thought to have been one of the state's best governors.

9. Richard A. Pettigrew (born June 10, 1930) was an American politician in the state of Florida. He attended the University of Florida and is an attorney. He was speaker of the Florida House of Representatives for the 97th district as a Democrat, serving from 1963 to 1972.

10. Earl Dewitt Hutto (born May 12, 1926) is an American politician. He is a former U.S. representative from Florida's 1st congressional district. Born in Midland City, Alabama, Hutto received a Bachelor of Science from Troy State University in 1949. Hutto was elected to the Florida House of Representatives in 1972 and was reelected in 1974 and 1976. He was elected as a Democrat to the 96th and to the seven succeeding congresses, serving from January 3, 1979, to January 3, 1995. He was not a candidate in 1994 for reelection to the 104th congress. Hutto was one of the most conservative Democrats in Congress during his tenure in office.

11. Pat Thomas (born in 1933) served as state senator from Quincy, Florida. A University of Florida graduate and Korean War veteran,

he served as chairman of the Florida Democratic Party from 1966 through 1970. He was elected to the Florida House in 1972, and the Florida Senate in 1974. He served as Senate president from 1993 to 1994. He died in 2000.

12. Thomas Terrell Sessums was born June 11, 1930, in Daytona Beach, Florida. Sessums graduated from the University of Florida with his Bachelor's degree and Juris Doctorate and began his law practice in Tampa. He served as a member of the Florida House of Representatives from 1963 until 1974. During the 1972-74 session he served as speaker of the House. He was also chairman of the Florida Board of Regents and is serving on the Board of Governors for Florida Southern College. He also served as president of the board of trustees at the University of Tampa.

13. The American Cancer Society's Reach to Recovery program has helped thousands of people cope with their breast cancer experience. When people first find out they have breast cancer, they may feel overwhelmed, vulnerable, and alone. While under this stress, many people must also learn about and try to understand complex medical treatments and then choose the best one. Talking with a specially trained Reach to Recovery volunteer at this time can give a measure of comfort and an opportunity for emotional grounding and informed decision-making. Volunteers are breast cancer survivors who give patients and family members an opportunity to express feelings, talk about their fears and concerns, and ask questions of someone who is knowledgeable and level-headed. Most importantly, Reach to Recovery volunteers offer understanding, support, and hope because they themselves have survived breast cancer and gone on to live normal, productive lives. They give the patients an opportunity to discuss their fears and concerns with someone who has already experienced the trauma of breast cancer.

CHAPTER SEVEN

THE CAMPAIGN

1979–Campaigning with Bob Graham

As Wayne and Margie were making plans to retire from politics and go back to their farm in Jackson County, another leading legislator was also making plans, and those plans included Wayne Mixson. A popular leader of the liberal, urban-oriented, South Florida wing of the Florida Democratic Party, Bob Graham, was making plans to become governor. In his strategic planning he recognized that his political support was weakest in the more conservative, rural, northern half of Florida. He knew that this weakness could be shored up by choosing a recognized leader from that area as his running mate. Immediately Wayne Mixson's name came forward as an ideal candidate for his lieutenant governor. If they could unite their bases of support on a combined ticket for the governorship, it would be a formidable team that would have a high probability of victory. Wayne describes how it happened.

"I had always respected and liked Bob Graham. We both entered the Florida House of Representatives as freshmen in the class of 1967. Although Bob came from a prominent Dade County family and was raised in urban South Florida, while I was raised on a small South Alabama farm near the Florida Panhandle border, our opinions, philosophies, and attitudes were very comparable. We shared a deep interest in Florida's environment and the state education systems, and we both wanted to bring jobs and industries to the state. Bob was deeply involved in urban issues, and I was immersed in agricultural development. We made a good team.

"After he had served two terms in the House of Representatives, Bob succeeded in a run for the Florida Senate. After serving eight years in that chamber, in 1979 he decided to run for the governorship. In order to increase his statewide name recognition, and as a means for evaluating his chances if he ran for the governorship, Graham embarked on a clever program which earned statewide media attention. In 1977 he began a 100-day work program, where he would join with the blue-collar citizens of Florida and share a workday with them. He worked as a bellhop, poop scooper, electrician's helper, lobster fisherman, dive boat deckhand, short-order cook, social worker, tomato picker, waiter, a night as a Tallahassee city policeman, and many other jobs. The public response was very favorable, and the media coverage was tremendous. The decision to seek the top state position was made.

"One of his most publicized workdays was when he joined the ranks of the homeless and unemployed. He was about to find out firsthand how badly the bureaucratic system treated some applicants. After working one day in St. Petersburg delivering furniture, for which he was paid twelve dollars, he used that money to pay for a night at the local Salvation Army Mission.

"The next day he was in the Tampa unemployment office attempting to file an application, when he needed to use the restroom. He found the door locked, and then was told it was for employees only, as proclaimed by a sign posted on the door. When he became governor, one of the first things he did was stop that restroom policy in state offices. He even secured that sign from the Tampa office and kept it on display in the governor's office. Today, the sign is still on display in his office in Dade County.

"The following day he continued in this role as he went to apply for food stamps. After walking the streets of Tampa during a hard rain, a drenched Bob Graham stood before the clerk's window as the clerk chewed on a big wad of chewing gum. When he asked for help in filling out the form, she rolled her eyes in disgust. It was an embarrassing experience for the state senator, but it made him appreciate how cruel the system could be to those it pretended to serve. The lesson made him much more sensitive to the needs of the poor. I thought that it was an ingenious approach to entering the campaign.

"Graham looked toward North Florida for a running mate, hoping to balance his appeal to a wider base of voters. He had made this decision six months before the end of qualifying, which was the traditional time that these decisions were announced. During all of our prior legislative interaction, I had never dreamed that our careers would be linked in a run for the governorship of the state of Florida."

Decision Time

"Bob Graham and I represented two vastly differing constituencies. He was from urban South Florida, and I was from rural North Florida. He had always been very active in promoting issues involving urban development, education, and the environment. Graham was also a farmer. They had a sizable family-owned and -operated Angus cattle operation in South Georgia, and a dairy farm in Graves County, Florida. That was a common bond between our backgrounds.

"I realized that I was under consideration as Bob Graham's choice for his lieutenant governor running mate. One clue was when my banker asked me why so many inquiries regarding my financial history were coming to him. Rumors were circulating in the capitol about Bob's choice, and my name was frequently at the forefront as a potential running mate for Bob Graham, or along with Bob Shevin,[1] who had also decided to run for the governorship. Meanwhile, I was preparing to announce my retirement from the House of Representatives and return to the farm.

"It all surfaced when Bob Graham phoned and asked me to meet him in Tampa. We met for several hours, discussing the potential a combined ticket would offer, our chances for success, our opposition, strategies, opportunities, potential problems, and other important factors of the endeavor. We also discussed similarities and differences in our philosophies, areas of interest, and opinions. Through his political career Bob had exhibited approaches which were skewed to the left, labeling him as a liberal.

"Conversely, I had generally leaned to the right, favoring the moderate or conservative views. Before beginning any alliance, I felt it was important that he and I both discuss and reach agreement on how we would handle these differences.

"We discussed several issues which we knew would arise during our term if we were victorious. We wanted to be sure that we were able to come to agreement on our positions on these matters. Bob wanted to change the selection process for the Florida Public Service Commission to an appointed system from the current elected commission system which I had favored. The same issue of how to best select candidates existed in the selection system for the governor's cabinet. I felt Florida's system of electing the cabinet was unique, especially since we were the only state that had the system prescribed in its state constitution. Through election the individual cabinet members realized greater power, while under an appointment system, the governor's position held more power. We eventually developed a compromise approach in which some of the positions are elected and others appointed. I emphasized to Bob that my main intent for running was to become instrumental in creating jobs in Florida.

"Bob and I represented two distinctly different constituencies. Since he was from the urban South, he worked to enhance agriculture, economic development, migrant worker living, and working conditions and housing for the poor. After discussing these issues in depth, we mutually agreed we could work together as a team, leading an administration with these issues in the forefront. As we left that meeting we realized that our alliance was formed, and the 'Graham-Cracker' ticket was in the race for the governorship.

"I was flattered by the opportunity Bob was offering me. Although I felt it was time for me to retire from the House of Representatives, the thought of moving to a top elected statewide position did appeal to me. I felt I was now well qualified for the task and hoped to accomplish much of what I felt was needed for the state. I still felt a deep desire to improve the state's environment for industry and thus bring valuable jobs to our citizens. I also wanted to assure this growth occurred with a minimum of collateral impact on our beautiful state.

"When I returned home, I discussed accepting Bob Graham's invitation with Margie. I explained that he came from a prominent South Florida family, graduated from the University of Florida, then from Harvard Law School as a Phi Beta Kappa, that we had resolved our potential areas of conflict, and he had agreed to support my economic and agricultural objectives. Most importantly, I told her we liked and respected each other, and I felt he was a man of principles and integrity. As usual she was willing to pitch in and work side by side with me through the effort. She said it would be a 'great way for us to go out.' Again, we were facing a major choice of directions on our life-journey together. We were embarking on an exciting, life-changing adventure!"

Making the Announcement

"Thursday, March 30, 1978, was a memorable day for us. It was the day that Bob Graham and I made our formal media announcements informing the public that we were seeking the Democratic nomination for the Governor-Lt. Governor positions. Almost immediately the papers cleverly named our ticket the 'Graham-Cracker' ticket. In a whirlwind of presentations, Bob and his wonderful wife, Adele, along with Margie and I, made public announcements on that day in Pensacola, Marianna, Tallahassee, Orlando, and Miami. As Bob introduced me as his running mate, he informed the media that my main roles would be economic development, liaison between the executive branch and the legislature, and coordination between state government and local governments across the state.

"Graham also pledged to continue his campaign promise to work at 100 different jobs across the state to better inform himself of the problems of the working citizens of the state. He added me to that pledge, stating that I would be working at jobs within local governments to better familiarize myself in that venue. Also, he pledged that neither of us would miss any legislative sessions because of our campaigning activities, since we both had near perfect attendance records. Our work had begun!

"Many of the recognized authorities on Florida politics predicted that the crowded Democratic race for the governorship would come down to a run-off between the Graham-Mixson pairing and the Shevin-Glisson ticket. Robert Shevin had chosen another North Florida representative as his running mate, James Glisson.[2] Remarkably, Glisson was originally from Jackson County, although he represented the 11th Florida district and resided in Tavares, Florida. They made an impressive opposing team. Our task was not going to be easy.

"Right away I realized that running for a statewide position, especially the governorship, was much different from campaigning for the state representative position in a single district. The scope of the job was much, much larger, and the competition was much, much more intense. This campaign was going to involve a lot of hard work. It had to include building a good campaign team. In order for us to win this campaign we would have to defeat a crowded field of Democratic contenders for the party nomination, and then in the final election defeat a tough Republican team."

Wayne and Margie had now enlisted in another exciting adventure. They were about to hit the campaign trail at a new level of intensity as they traveled the width and length of the state of Florida, attending events, working with the media at every opportunity, and making thousands of new friends.

The ballot for the primary was going to include the following declared tickets:

Democratic Nomination for Governor and Lieutenant Governor

Bob Graham and Wayne Mixson
Claude Kirk and Mary Singleton
Robert Shevin and Jim Glisson
Bruce Smathers and Charles Boyd
Hans Tanzler and Manuel Arques
Jim Williams and Betty Castor
LeRoy Eden and Maria Kay

Republican Nomination for Governor and Lieutenant Governor

Jack Eckerd and Paula Hawkins
Lou Frey Jr. and Peter Capua

Wayne recalls his feelings as he faced this new challenge: "This broad field of candidates included one former governor, one former lieutenant governor, one U.S. representative, one former Florida secretary of state, one former Florida attorney general, one former state legislator, one mayor, and two businessmen. It was a slate filled with talented, powerful people. They were going to be tough to beat.

"I was given a big emotional boost when, within a few days of our initial announcement, the *Jackson County Floridan* and Guy Long, the president of the local Jackson County Chapter of the N.A.A.C.P., both made publicized endorsements of the Graham-Mixson ticket. Guy Long held a press conference to proclaim his support for our campaign. He stated that he wanted to dispel any claims that I was just another redneck racist from North Florida. He said that he felt that I was the exact opposite of that stereotype. In all of his dealings with me during my many terms in the legislature, I had always been fair, ethical, unbiased, and responsive to what was needed. He said he felt I held a deep desire to help the poor and needy citizens of the state.

"Also, immediately after the announcement, the *Papoose*, which was the campus news bulletin at Chipola Junior College where Margie taught English, ran a story about our run for the governorship. In the item it noted how Margie's life was about to go through a major change if she became the wife of the lieutenant governor of Florida, instead of being a regular instructor at Chipola. Along with carrying a heavy instruction workload, Margie was also the president of the faculty Senate. She had been teaching at the college level for twelve years, one year longer than I had served in the legislative branch.

"As she entered the campaign, the article noted that she would be trading her test papers and lecture notes for 'peanuts and Graham crackers.' Her waking hours will be filled with receptions, teas, meetings, luncheons, coffees, and banquets. The article included a statement from Margie that she was eagerly anticipating opportunities to help me during the campaigning.

"Another article in the *Jackson County Floridan* noted how Margie's attitude about politicians had changed since I first talked with her about running for the state representative seat back in 1966. At that time, she said she was 'horrified' at the prospect of me becoming a politician. She said that people said such bad things about politicians, and she could not stand the thought of people saying bad things about me. However, when the prospect of me becoming the lieutenant governor was discussed she stated that she was 'very excited,' and was eager to pitch in and help with the campaigning. However, she noted that she would not be available until the current college session was completed. 'My attitude about politicians has definitely changed,' she was quoted.

"The article also went on to note her other activities outside of a busy campus regimen. This included her work as a Sunday school teacher, her position on the administrative board of the First Methodist Church in Marianna, her work on the board of directors of the Jackson County American Cancer Society, and chairmanship of cancer drives.

"The story went on to note that Margie and I had enjoyed a wonderful thirty-year-long marriage. (We celebrated seventy years of togetherness in December 2017.) The item related how we both respected each other's work, accomplishments, and career. It told of how we do not make demands of each other out of respect for our individual responsibilities, priorities, and duties. The story explained that we had developed a means of open, honest communication that was vital to the success of our marriage."

On the Campaign Trail

Then the campaigning began. Margie and Wayne were soon consumed by a rigorous schedule that was designed to keep them in the public eye. Wayne continues his description: "The ensuing weeks and months became a whirlwind of events, speeches, discussions, introductions, and handshaking. I enjoyed it immensely, even though it involved hours and hours of work and travel, nights in strange beds, and too much catered food. When you are required to give repeated presentations before varied groups on a concentrated schedule, you soon develop a basic routine for your speeches.

"I usually began with recognition of those who were sponsoring the event, my appreciation for the opportunity to take part, a humorous anecdote or two, and a short dissertation on what were the basic objectives of the Graham-Mixson administration. These included programs to enhance education, provide housing for the poor, protection of the environment, increased industrial recruitment, creation of jobs, protection of the state's agricultural interest, more local control, and openness and honesty in government. I always ended by asking for their votes and support. I'm not saying it was a 'canned' speech; it was flavored with local relevance, but the core message and general form were usually the same, and it was always well received.

"For me, the first week was the worst week of the entire campaign. I had to develop a list of prospects from all of the many people I considered friends, those I had worked with, and those I knew, and others our research had identified as people and organizations who were potential supporters of our campaign. Then I had to call each of them and solicit their support. I spent an entire week with telephone in hand, making these calls.

"I did not concentrate on agricultural areas of the state. It was assumed that we were going to do very well in rural areas. I spent most of my time scheduled for events in urban areas. Heavy emphasis was placed on Lee County, Southwest Florida, and on the I-4 corridor from Tampa to Volusia County. I also worked the condominiums in Broward County. I remember I was in the home of John Leban, the chairman of the Broward County Democratic Committee, preparing for an evening meeting when the announcement came on television that Ronald Reagan had been shot.

"Scheduling was a constant area of focus and concern. Often we had conflicting demands for our presence on the same date at locations hundreds of miles apart. Most of the time, by using the speaking skills of Margie, Adele, Bob, and myself, we were able to cover the demands. While the 1978 legislature was in session, we gave priority to fulfilling our legislative duties.

"There was one occasion where our scheduling coordinator made an error, and I was confirmed to be in two locations at the same time. One was an important event in Quincy where I was supposed to debate our Republican opponent, Paula Hawkins. The other was a scheduled speech before the Taylor County Cattleman's Association event in Perry. At the last minute we realized the problem and made arrangements for Margie to represent me in Perry at the Cattleman's dinner, while I fulfilled the Quincy obligation.

"Although Margie had little forewarning and little time to prepare, she gamely agreed to be my stand-in at the event. I quickly gave her an outline of the material I would have presented if I had been able to go. As Margie started giving the speech, she found that she covered all of my notes within the first ten minutes. In order to fill the remaining time, she switched topics and gave a presentation on what life was like on the campaign trail. The crowd loved it and gave her a standing ovation. I think they ended up happier with what she delivered than they would have been with my dissertation. Margie came through and averted what could have been an unfortunate situation for our campaign.

"On another occasion Margie was faced with a similar situation when she had to substitute for me at a barbeque in Madison which was being hosted by the local sheriff. She was picked up and flown to Madison in a small airplane. Madison did not have an airport, so the pilot announced that they were going to land in a nearby field. He asked Margie to help him be sure there were no cattle in the way as they did a fly-by before landing. Thankfully, there were no cows in the way, so they landed safely. A pickup truck arrived and drove her to the home of the sheriff. Margie gave another memorable speech, and the event was a success for us all.

"It was mid-May and we were into our second month after the announcement when a humorous blooper gained us statewide notoriety. During an early morning newscast, a reporter for radio station WSUN in the Tampa-St. Petersburg area was relating how Miami Lakes state senator, Bob Graham, had chosen Wayne Mixson, a North Florida marijuana farmer, as his running mate. A few minutes later the embarrassed announcer corrected himself and explained that he meant to say, 'Marianna farmer,' and apologized for his error.

"Of course, almost every newspaper in the state picked up the item after it was first written by Hampton Dunn and published in the "Florida Explorer," the publication for the Florida Peninsula Motor Club.[3] The *Pensacola Journal* even had a large cartoon depicting a hippie radio announcer at a radio station console, smoking pot and making the announcement. One paper suggested that we should change the ticket slogan from the 'Graham-Cracker' ticket to the 'Graham-Grass' ticket. I thought it was quite funny, and realized that it had gained us a tremendous amount of free publicity across the state. When the spring session of the 1978 Florida legislature approached its conclusion and my retirement became a reality, I was showered with articles and expressions of appreciation from my peers in the legislature, agricultural interests across the state, and many constituents from my District Seven home base. It was a humbling experience.

"I was recognized for eight years of service as chairman of the House Agriculture Committee and membership on the House Rules Committee. During the last week of the session, I was honored to receive a special recognition award from the combined agricultural industries and associations in the state. I will forever treasure this wonderful tribute and the kind words of praise embossed on the beautiful plaque which I was presented.

"Another recognition I was given during that last week of the session was a 'Letter of Tribute' which was read on the House floor by Speaker Donald Tucker.[4] Public tributes were also made by many of my friends and supporters in District Seven. These included noted farmers and businessmen, such as Howard Odom in Marianna, R. D. Bennett of Greenwood, H. D. Hagler of Malone, Rudolph Rackley of Altha, Dr. T J. Culpepper of Marianna, David Locke of Graceville, and others. It all overwhelmed me, and I will always remain humbled by their praise."

Goodbye Legislature, Hello Campaigning

"With my final legislative session behind us, in June, Bob and I were able to turn full attention to our campaign. At this time there were less than 100 days left before the September 12 primary, and I was tasked with visiting all sixty-seven Florida counties before that date. Also, it was planned for me to engage in several 'workdays' at various county offices around the state in order to stress my involvement with local governments and for increased familiarization with operations and difficulties within local governments in Florida. My visitation and speaking engagements were tilted toward the southern portion of Florida, since I was already well known throughout most of North Florida.

"In an endless array of talks and interviews I remained focused on the issues which I felt deserved my concern. These were heavy taxation, especially as related to property taxes, my belief that education funding should be primarily derived through sources other than property taxation, my ongoing opposition to a state income tax, my concerns related to the constant growth in the size and cost of government, increased regulations, the need for better relationships between the state government and county and municipal governments in Florida, the need for a much more active and meaningful state Department of Commerce to work with local officials in a combined effort to entice and locate new job-producing, clean industries, my belief in capital punishment, opposition to casino gambling, ongoing work to improve housing for the poor, improved working conditions for migrant workers, favoring an elected cabinet and, of course, improving Florida's agricultural industries. As you can see, there was no shortage of subject material for my speaking engagements."

On Monday, June 12, Margie and Wayne pulled out of Marianna in a Winnebago which had been loaned to them by Bob Graham. They were starting a week-long campaign swing through Central Florida. Wayne clearly remembers the events of that trip. "We were scheduled to visit numerous radio and newspaper media all along the route. Margie had no teaching duties at Chipola College during the summer session, so our campaigning created no conflicts for her. We were both excited about the adventure and the opportunity to meet so many new people.

"After a stop in Lake City for an interview with the local media and a visit with some old Farm Bureau friends, we attended an afternoon reception in Gainesville. Then on Tuesday and Wednesday we continued the tour through several towns south of that city. On Thursday we swung back northward, up into the Panhandle, and continued through several Panhandle cities. Finally, we ended up back in Marianna. The whistle-stop trip was a good start for both of us and certainly got us into the campaigning spirit."

Wayne's unique background experience became a valuable asset during the campaign. His long relationship with Farm Bureau, and his familiarity with leaders of all elements of Florida's agricultural community, opened many opportunities for their campaigning activities. Wayne recalls how this aided their efforts. "Another important voting group that was my responsibility was the large citrus farm industry in central Florida. Several of our competitors also had strong alliances in this arena and were working for their support. During my last legislative session, I had been instrumental in getting a bill passed through both chambers which provided for giving tax rebates to these farmers for citrus advertising.

"Before my involvement, the bill had been defeated in the Senate and had little chance of passage. I found the most effective way of appealing to them was to look them straight in the eye and ask, 'Of those running for governor, which team has done the most for your business during the past ten years?' There was only one answer they could honestly give to that question.

"Early in July our campaign was energized by our supporters in Jackson County. They organized a fundraising fish fry for our ticket at the Jackson County Agricultural Center and a huge crowd turned out for the event. Over 2,000 plates loaded with fish and trimmings were served. During the afternoon the Marianna Woman's Club held a reception honoring Margie and Adele. It was a great day for all four of us.

"Fairly early in the campaign I campaigned for a whole week in Southwest Florida. Using Fort Myers as a base, we worked the area daily. One night at a community rally I was introduced by Johnny Cash and his wife, June Carter Cash. That was a big boost and I went behind the stage to meet and visit with them. The last night of that week Bob came down and we had a huge rally. Senator Frank Mann and many other legislators helped organize this event. Our many friends in the Florida legislature, both the House and the Senate, were very helpful to us throughout the campaign. Another great occasion was with Bill Buckley at one of his well-attended lectures. I had a good visit with him, and he introduced me to the crowd.

"Margie and I were both astounded by the unending enthusiasm, generosity, assistance, and kindness which was extended to us everywhere we went as we campaigned. Volunteers whom we did not know lodged us, fed us, flew us, drove us, and did everything possible to assist us in our efforts. We had numerous airplanes at our disposal which were offered by supporters who were aircraft owners and pilots. Mariana businessman, Howard Odom, loaned us his personal airplane for a full week, and movie star and FSU graduate, Burt Reynolds, sent us his helicopter and pilot to use. During the entire campaign there was not a single instance in which we had to ride in a taxi. It was an amazing and enlightening experience for both of us. I recall looking out of an airplane window one night as we flew over South Florida, looking at all of the lights and thinking, 'How are we ever going to meet all of those people?'

"July became a blur of events, festivals, banquets, photo opportunities, interviews, and speeches. During the month we visited almost forty counties across the state. Notable activities included participating in the Monticello Watermelon Festival and a workday in Marianna. On this workday Bob and I assisted in a project which involved moving a donated house onto a parcel of land, and preparing the property and building to become a new senior citizen center for the Marianna community. It was a good project and we also earned some great press from our participation. In one three-day period during July, I was scheduled for eleven stops in ten different counties.

"July started with its traditional 'bang' on the fourth of the month, and for the Graham-Mixson campaign it ended with a bang with a huge fundraising rally in Okeechobee. We traveled to the Okeechobee Agricultural Center the last Saturday in July for a barbeque which drew over 4,000 people from all over the state. We were overwhelmed with the turnout. Caravans reportedly came from around fifty counties in Florida. Chartered buses from

South Florida, campers, pickup trucks, and cars filled the parking area.

"Okeechobee is located in the middle of the South Florida farming district, and the turnout from that sector was huge. The event was done in a traditional, down-home theme and featured great musical entertainment, games for the children, speeches, and great food. We barbequed 2,000 pounds of beef along with wild hogs and swamp cabbage. It was fun and exciting, and was a tremendous display of support for our drive for the governorship. Also during July, Bob announced that when we took office he would form a special taxation evaluation committee, with me as the chairman. The purpose of this committee would be to evaluate the negative impact that the existing taxes and regulations were having on Florida's industries, businesses, and individuals. He stated that we would seek to limit the cost of supporting schools at the local level to around 25 percent and increase state support of the cost of education. These ideas were well received across the state."

It was at this point in the increasingly competitive campaign that Wayne and Bob incurred some negative publicity created by their opponents. Wayne relates how that unjustified and untrue remark impacted him, and how Margie helped them overcome the negative effect. "August is the month for the annual Wausau Possum Festival, and of course we were there. It was also the month that I encountered a very disturbing, negative situation which arose from competitive campaigning. An article in the *Miami Herald* quoted Jim Glisson, Robert Shevin's running mate, as saying that I had made a 'racial remark' during a conversation with him. He claimed that I had used a terrible racial slur when I discussed getting the black vote to come out.

"I vigorously denied and corrected the quote, but I felt damage to our effort had been realized. It was difficult to accept the possibility that the Shevin campaign was resorting to unethical tactics, but I knew Glisson's story was not true. Within the next few days two publicized events helped in the restoration of faith in our honor and unbiased philosophies. We immediately began to take corrective action to this slur.

"First, Margie had a black minister in one of her classes at Chipola College. The week before the Glisson story was released, he had invited Margie to speak before his congregation. Margie arrived at the church early and the young pastor took her into his study, and they prayed together. Then Margie was introduced before the congregation. She gave a talk about the campaign and how our faith had always led us in our legislative work. She emphasized that our belief in God would continue to guide me if I became lieutenant governor. Then she was overjoyed as many of the black leaders who were among those in attendance began to stand and give testimony about how I had always been a friend and ally to the poor, and the black community. The event was widely covered by the media and was a big step in healing the wounds created by the *Miami Herald* story.

"Then within a few days I was asked to be interviewed during a news program at a Panama City television station. I gave a heartfelt rendition of my emotional concern for the displaced workers, those with need for better housing, more good jobs, and education. It was one of the best presentations I have ever given. We received a lot of positive feedback from black leadership as a result of that exposure.

"Bob Graham, along with many of my lifelong friends and supporters, all made public statements affirming the fact that I would never engage in derogatory racial remarks. They noted that throughout my political career I had demonstrated concern and compassion for the poor and the middle class. I deeply appreciated the fact that they quickly rose to defend me. When all of the dust settled from this dirt-throwing, we felt we had restored the faith of the minority voters."

As the primary elections neared, their anxieties grew. Wayne discusses some of their strategies in this latter phase of the campaign: "Political polling conducted during mid-August claimed that we were running second to the Shevin-Glisson ticket, but were closing the gap. As planned, I continued to concentrate most of my time solidifying our support in the agricultural sector, while Bob worked in the more liberal urban areas. With seven candidates vying for the governorship, it was almost a sure bet that, in the September 12 primary vote, none of the tickets would get a majority vote. This would then require a run-off between the top two finishers. We wanted to be sure we were one of those two top tickets.

"I was very happy when the Panhandle Production Credit Association[5] published a front-page feature story about me and the Graham-Cracker ticket in the August issue of their monthly paper, the 'Panhandle Farmer.' This publication was distributed to farmers throughout North Florida and the Panhandle. The story reviewed my career, my service on the Agriculture Committee, legislation which I had sponsored which aided Florida's farmers, and the various agricultural awards I had been given through the years. It ended with an endorsement of our ticket.

"On August 20, in a glowing editorial, the *Tallahassee Democrat* endorsed our ticket for the election which was only four weeks away at that point. The article gave a very positive review of the accomplishments we both achieved during our legislative careers, it praised our honesty and integrity, and included a review of our campaign platform. It stressed that, because of our experience and diversity, we would do a good job of representing all of Florida, both rural and urban.

"Many of the events we attended during the months of campaigning were fun. I recall one occasion at Florida A&M when the Florida Grape Growers held a 'stomp' at the FAMU Perry-Paige Auditorium. The politicians in attendance were divided into stomping teams, which stood barefooted in a barrel of grapes and vigorously stomped the grapes for two minutes. The team which produced the most juice was the winner. It was one of those rare times when physical weight was better than political weight. Having big feet was also an important factor. I didn't win, but I had a great time. A picture of me stomping energetically in a big sombrero was published in the media.

"On September 1 the *Jackson County Floridan* gave us a great endorsement in a well-written editorial. The feature stressed our intent to assist the seniors, poor, and middle class with property tax relief. It also discussed our intent to limit the local burden in funding education. Additionally, the editorial detailed our promised 'Florida Tax Reform Commission' which I would chair while we searched for ways to engage in tax reform measures. It also described our intent to develop programs to aid the growing elderly population across Florida. We also received strong endorsements from several other newspapers, including the *Fort Lauderdale News*, *Miami News*, and *St. Petersburg Times*.

"Our strategist designed an elaborate ranking system in order to assure that throughout the campaign we allocated our valuable time on a basis which gave us a balanced exposure across the state. The system divided the state into seven sections and gave points on a weighted basis for events we attended in each section.

"By the time the campaign ended I had visited all sixty-seven counties in Florida, and Margie had visited all but three or four of them. We felt that we knew Florida's geography and its climates, physical and philosophical. The final week of the campaign came and passed at an even faster pace. Finally, September 12 arrived. It was election day in Florida."

Voting Day—The September Primary

"On election night we were with friends and supporters as we waited for the final vote count to be announced. Bob and Adele hosted a similar event in Miami. In Tallahassee, we had about 300 supporters with us during the anxious wait. I was praying for two outcomes. First, I wanted the Graham-Mixson ticket to finish in first or second place so that we would be in the October 5 run-off election, and second, I wanted to trounce Jim Glisson in

Jackson County, since he had bragged that he was going to be the victor in my home county.

"My prayers were answered in both instances. Bob and I finished a strong second statewide, with the Shevin-Glisson ticket receiving 354,222 votes, while Bob and I had 255,685 votes. We won all but one county throughout North Florida. In Jackson County we swamped the Shevin-Glisson team, with Bob and me getting 6,335 votes to their 774. The folks back home had come through for Margie and me.

"Now we had four weeks of head-to-head campaigning ahead of us until the October 5 vote. The focus now turned to capturing those voters who had supported the five losing tickets. We knew that we would now be able to obtain donations which we could use to expand our statewide advertising. We designed an advertising program intended to impact areas where those needed transfer votes existed. We felt we had a good chance to win the upcoming runoff.

"New endorsements and financial supporters immediately began to appear. Everyone realized that there was a good probability the Graham-Mixson team would win the election for governor of Florida. In Escambia County the existing Pensacola mayor, the city's prior mayor, and several top business leaders all announced their support for our ticket. They had previously supported Jim Williams. Another group of Pensacola businessmen who had previously been staunch supporters of Smathers came into our camp. In late September the Jacksonville *Florida Times-Union* and *Port St. Joe Star* announced their endorsements for our effort in very complimentary editorials. As more and more announcements were made pledging support for us, our excitement grew.

"The week before the election a televised debate between Bob Graham and Robert Shevin was held in Tampa. Bob was in good form and did a great job of arguing and explaining our philosophies and platform. As our momentum grew, it seemed that our competitors became more aggressive out of desperation. At the debate, Shevin violated the designated rules by repeatedly interrupting while Bob was making rebuttals to his arguments. Then Shevin was booed when he launched a personal attack against Bob. Most people felt Bob won the contest.

"In another last-minute effort before the election, a paid thirty-minute program featuring Senators Childers of Pensacola and Dempsey Barron of Panama City appeared on a South Florida television station. In the program they blasted Bob Graham's voting record in the legislature. The dirt-throwing was intensifying as the campaigns were coming to a conclusion. It was about this time that five of the major television stations in South Florida refused to run several of Shevin's advertisements, after Bob provided proof of their inaccuracies. They were negatively attacking Bob's legislative voting record. I felt that the publicity about their questionable approaches backfired on the Shevin camp and hurt their image; and then election day was upon us.

"Suddenly it was October 5, another decision day for Florida voters. Margie and I voted during the morning and then went to a hotel in Tallahassee to wait for the results to come in. I was preparing a concession speech which I hoped would sound like I was losing in a gracious manner. I hoped I would not have to deliver it. I also made some notes which I could use as a victory speech, in case we won.

"That evening our suite was filled with excitement as the results began to be announced across the state. For what seemed an eternity the tallies were close, then our totals began to mount. When 100 percent of the vote was in, we were the winners! We had won by a 54 percent margin, with a 62,000 vote lead. It was the first time in state history a candidate who finished a primary in second place by more than 100,000 votes was able to come back and win. We were officially representing the Democratic Party in the upcoming general election.

"I was greatly gratified by the results which came in from my North Florida home base. We carried Jackson County by a margin of 7,324 votes to 1,777. The folks back home had come through for us once again."

Down the Final Stretch

"There was no time to pause and rest. The final elections were set for November 7, which was only four weeks away. We had to plan our activities, advertising, and plan of engagement for the powerful Republican ticket we were opposing. We were now just one hurdle away from the final goal—the Florida governor's office. The only thing standing in our way was the Republican team of Jack Eckerd[6] and Paula Hawkins. Once again we were facing a difficult task. Many of the people who had previously backed the Shevin-Glisson ticket publicly announced that they were now supporting Graham-Mixson. We even picked up two supporters who had been major backers for Republican Lou Frey when he ran against Eckerd and Hawkins. The state Democratic family was quickly consolidating its support for us.

"In a speech before the Florida Citrus Growers, Bob Graham outlined the role that he intended his lieutenant governor to play in his administration. 'He will play an important dual role,' he said. 'He will develop the state economic policy to assure that the state begins to play a supportive role to local efforts to create economic development, new industrial recruitment, and creation of new jobs in needed areas. He will form the liaison between local governments and the state.'

"He went on to state that neither of us was satisfied with the effort which had historically been demonstrated by the state to help local communities in economic development efforts. He also stressed the need to continue to enhance growth in existing industries, such as agriculture. 'Wayne Mixon and I are a team,' he concluded. I was looking forward to the job.

"September passed in a blur of barbeques, fish fries, and banquets, as requests for our presence multiplied tremendously. At many of these events, Margie and Adele wore dresses which were covered with green printing proclaiming the Graham-Cracker ticket. Their 'Graham for Governor' attire was becoming a recognized symbol of our campaign.

"When Bob and I both spoke at a major campaign event, we made what I felt was a compelling presentation. Bob would describe his legislative career, with his focus on controlling and managing urban development, and his ongoing work to preserve the environment of Florida. His record of sponsoring environmental legislation included the Clean Water Constitutional Amendment of 1970, the Environmental Protection Act of 1971, the Land and Water Management Act of 1972, the State Comprehensive Planning Act of 1972, the Environmentally Endangered Lands and Outdoor Recreation Bond Issue of 1972, the Big Cypress Conservation Act of 1973, and the Local Government Comprehensive Planning Act of 1974.

"Then during my presentation I would describe my work to hold the line on property tax increases, the creation of the homestead exemption, my work to fund a major portion of the cost of local schools from state funds, my work to improve housing for the poor, my interest in the environment, and most of all my work to enhance state industrial recruitment programs, to work with local efforts for jobs creation, and my plans to create a meaningful Department of Commerce within the state organization.

"I often discussed removal of the hardships placed on local governments by the state practice of often issuing unfunded mandates, and by what I termed 'suck-along tactics.' This term describes the state practice of promoting a new service or system through initial 'cost sharing' of the cost, with the state paying a major portion and the local government paying a smaller portion. Then, in the ensuing years, the state removes or significantly reduces its funding, thus leaving the local government footing the bill. By the time Bob and I had detailed most of these subjects, we usually had the support of our audience.

"One of the highlights of the last stretch of our campaign was a huge fish fry which was put on by my loyal supporters in Jackson County. On Saturday, September 28, at the Marianna Farm Center, over 2,000 people assembled to visit with Bob and me to express their support, and to listen to our stories. It was a great evening of homecoming for me. Meanwhile, Republicans Jack Eckerd and Paula Hawkins were also out on the trail in their rigorous campaign. Since at that time Democratic voter registrations in the state outnumbered Republicans by a 2-1 margin, they realized they would have to capture many crossover voters and undecided voters. They also knew they had to score well in North and Central Florida to overcome the South Florida urban votes. Their campaign speeches and advertising emphasized that they were a more conservative choice, as they described Bob's legislative history as a demonstration of liberalism. 'We promote Management of Government, instead of Expansion of Government,' was one of their slogans. I must state that throughout their campaign, Jack Eckerd maintained a high level of ethics, respect, and restraint in the competition. He raised the level of campaign behavior. Many praised us for also remaining on the high ground.

"Several newspapers wrote articles which noted that the main defense our ticket had against these claims was the 'presence of Wayne Mixson' on Graham's ticket. The articles stated that my record was much more conservative in emphasis on enhancing local governments, creating jobs, controlling taxation, and promoting agricultural needs. They proclaimed that the Graham-Mixson combination created a well-balanced choice.

"Campaigning at this point seemed to change from whirlwind speed to full hurricane force. In Hillsborough County over 3,000 seniors attended a luncheon honoring Adele Graham for numerous senior programs she had helped to foster, including Meals on Wheels. Two big events were held in Dade County as fundraisers for our campaign. One featured a performance by Jimmy Buffet, who sang several songs at Monty Trainer's in Miami. The event raised over $40,000. Then the next day the campaign moved onto the ocean on a new cruise ship. Six hundred supporters enjoyed an entertaining, luxurious evening cruise which raised about $110,000. By the end of the campaign, donations for our run for the state's top position raised over $3,000,000.

"Brevard County hosted two fundraisers, one at Melbourne Century Country Club, and the other at Fox Lake Park Pavilion. Broward County hosted a big breakfast on September 22, which I attended. In Lee County Bob spoke before a large crowd at the Port Charlotte Cultural Center. Then on the same day he spoke before five hundred people in Pinellas County at the Top of the World, which is the largest condominium project in the nation. On October 4, Leon County held a huge barbeque across from the Hilton Hotel in Lewis Park. Additionally, on October 2, a twelve-county fish fry was held at the Suwannee County Coliseum in Live Oak. The title given the event was 'Friends to Elect Graham-Mixson.' Over five thousand folks attended. Whew!!

"As election day approached, Eckerd won the endorsement of the influential mayor of Jacksonville, Hans Tanzler.[7] He had promised Tanzler a position as chairman of a local government advisory committee if he was elected governor. Tanzler had previously been president of the Florida League of Cities, so this committee was an area of interest for him. They made the announcement at the annual convention of the League of Cities.

"Bob counteracted this announcement by reiterating his promise that I would chair a similar position as the primary liaison between state government and local governments. Also, he reminded the media that he was immediately going to form a committee, which would be chaired by me, with the mission of reviewing all state taxes on individuals and businesses, and that I would lead in the creation of meaningful industrial development programs in the state. He promised that the League of Cities would be asked to send a representative to serve on the taxation review committee.

He also promised to work to prevent more unfunded mandates from the state being imposed on local governments.

"During October the state Democratic Party held a huge 'Unity Dinner,' which was organized to demonstrate the strength and unification of all of the leaders of the party behind the Graham-Cracker ticket, as well as for George Firestone, who was running for secretary of state. The event was filled with former governors, powerful state legislators, and leading private supporters. A highlight during the event for us was an emotional endorsement which was publicly bestowed by Robert Shevin.

Paula Hawkins Attacks Graham

"On October 23, the *Tampa Times* published a glowing endorsement for Bob and me. It lauded our high level of experience, our balanced offering, and the history of political ethics which both of us had demonstrated during our prior service. It also compared my qualifications to the qualifications of Paula Hawkins, describing some of her decisions on the Public Service Commission as 'irresponsible.' It also discussed the fact that the 65-year-old Eckerd had some health problems which increased the possibility of his being replaced by Hawkins if a tragedy occurred. It stated that I was better qualified to serve as a governor, and that since Bob was only 41, the potential for a succession was greatly diminished. This powerful endorsement helped us in Central Florida.

"On October 26, the *Miami Herald* published a story describing an exchange between Paula Hawkins and Bob Graham at a West Palm Beach Chamber of Commerce breakfast. It was intentionally designed to be a debate. On the same speaking program, the event featured Jack Eckerd, Bob Graham, Paula Hawkins, and me. Everyone anxiously awaited the fireworks.

"Jack Eckerd and Bob Graham were the first to speak. Jack Eckerd promised to attract 'high technology, non-polluting' industries to Florida by improving the universities, 'rolling out the welcome mat,' cutting regulatory red tape, and enlisting a cadre of Florida's top businessmen to assist in recruitment. He blamed Florida's poor performance in industrial development as compared to neighboring states on a prevailing anti-business attitude, and a tax-and-spend attitude in the legislature.

"Bob delivered his usual dissertation on his legislative accomplishments relating to preservation of the environment, enhancing education, restraining taxation, and emphasizing the creation of new, desirable jobs. He also outlined our plans to freeze all new taxes while a detailed review was conducted, to improve communications and coordination between the state and local governments, and to build a strong, effective Department of Commerce to usher in a strong push to bring jobs to Florida. He included a remark that steps needed to be taken to control inflation, including a limit of the number of state employees to one percent of the state population; to freeze property taxes for two years by rolling back the millage to counter assessment increases; and to enact programs to increase competition in many markets.

"Next to speak was Paula Hawkins, and the much-awaited fireworks started. She began with, 'I tore up the speech I had prepared when I heard Bob Graham speak. I have a reputation for speaking out, and I am about to confirm that rumor.' For the next twenty minutes she delivered a scathing attack on Bob's voting record. She linked some of Bob's history of supporting government price supports on agricultural products to inflation, even blaming him for the high cost of milk. She called Bob's popular '100 workdays' a campaign gimmick. She chastised him for voting against a resolution which would have required an amendment to request a federal constitutional convention to require a balanced federal budget. Her tone and demeanor were very antagonistic. The speech won her a lot of media attention.

"I next rose to deliver my speech. I began by saying, 'I had a choice of whether to speak first or second. I chose second, and now I have to follow that! Can you believe that?' I then did my best to counter some of her most damaging statements, and to remind the attendees of my conservative, tax-restraining history. I also promoted our plans to spur new industrial growth and new jobs where they are needed in Florida. It was quite a morning for us, and a troubling way to start the day.

"Our campaign was again reinforced when, during the last week of October, President Carter flew to Florida to deliver his endorsement. It was during his Camp David Mideast Peace Accord, and his popularity was at a high point at that time. I had to leave the meeting with the president to speak at the annual meeting of the Panhandle Production Credit Association in Marianna. I opened that speech by proclaiming how amazing our world was today, when I could have been standing on a platform in Miami before a crowd of 15,000 with President Carter only two and a half hours ago, and now be in Marianna making a speech. I then discussed the importance of agriculture to Florida's economy, the problems the industry was facing, and programs that were needed to cultivate agriculture in the state. I was graciously given a standing ovation at the beginning and, more importantly, again at the end of my talk.

"On Friday, October 27, the folks of Jackson County did it again. They organized a Wayne Mixson Appreciation Day barbecue at the Farm Center. It looked as if everyone in the area came to the event, as Margie and I were showered with compliments and expressions of support by an estimated crowd of 3,000 people. Bob had cancelled one of his scheduled events to be there for the barbecue. He delivered a speech which included a glowing expression of his appreciation for my contributions to his campaign. He even made an attempt to sing our campaign song as a tribute to Margie and me. He said he hoped his singing wouldn't cost us any votes. Astoundingly, the event raised approximately $30,000 for our campaign effort.

"As election day continued to approach, on November 2 the influential *Orlando Sentinel Star* wrote a glowing editorial which endorsed us. It discussed the age and vitality differences between Graham and Eckerd and their philosophical differences, and offered a comparison between Paula and me. It stated that, although it appreciated Paula's consumer activism, they felt she was not the 'tactful non-partisan diplomat' that Jack Eckerd would need at his side.

"The next day I was one of the designated ribbon cutters for the opening of a public facility in Pensacola. Governor Askew was also there. As I struggled to cut the ribbon, Askew quipped that I needed to get a bigger pair of scissors if I planned to cut the size of government while I was lieutenant governor. It was funny and made good press for us.

"On the eve of the election, November 6, the *Tallahassee Democrat* published another significant endorsement for the Graham-Cracker ticket. They also endorsed Jackson County's Don Fuqua who was running for U.S. representative. Election was upon us!"

November 7, Election Day!

"On election day an article in the *Tampa Tribune* heralded the event and encouraged everyone to vote. It anticipated that some 2.3 million Floridians would turn out, and described the ballot as including choices for a new governor and lieutenant governor, cabinet positions, legislative positions at the state and federal levels, and issues such as casino gambling and several significant constitutional revisions. It also stated that last-minute polls predicted that our ticket would win.

"During the morning, Margie and I voted in Marianna and then traveled to Miami to join Bob and Adele at the Miami Lakes Inn and Country Club for what we hoped would be a victory party. That evening we all watched anxiously as returns from across the state began to come in. We were at the end of what had been a long, eventful campaign trail."

WE WON!!

"It was a heavy voter turnout, which helped our vote count. In South Florida, the heavy turnout was partially attributed to the controversial casino gambling issue. It was a landslide victory, with Graham-Mixson getting 1.4 million votes and Eckerd-Hawkins getting 1.1 million votes, a 56 percent to 44 percent margin. In the Panhandle, it was a landslide for our team. In my beloved Jackson County, we were given the largest margin in the history of the county, an 8,160 to 1,621 vote victory.

"Early in the evening Bob Graham received a congratulatory phone call from President Carter. 'Congratulations, Governor Graham,' he exclaimed. After he had concluded the call, Bob plopped into a lounge chair and said, 'Whew! That is the first time I ever received a phone call from a president to call me governor.'

"It seemed almost unbelievable to me that I was about to be the lieutenant governor of Florida. Margie and I hugged each other, overcome with excitement and joy. When I was interviewed by the media, I commented that we had formed a great team which had been in 'full court press' for months. It was an exciting evening of celebration and giving thanks to the hundreds of people who had helped us win."

Coming Home

"We began the following day with Bob and me standing at one of the busiest intersections in Miami, holding signs which read, 'Thank You, People of Florida!' After lunch we went to the airport and boarded a waiting jet for our return to Jackson County, arriving at the Marianna Airport around 4:00 p.m. A wonderful surprise awaited at our destination. Our local airport operator and Lear pilot, Harold Foran, parked our airplane on the Marianna ramp. As the passengers deplaned, including Margie and me; Margie's mother, Wilkie; County Commissioner, Durelle Johnson; and my sister Miriam, we were cheered by over 1,000 local citizens who had assembled and awaited our arrival. The

Marianna High School marching band serenaded us, and local beauty queens gave the women bouquets of roses. Marianna mayor, J. D. Swearingen, made a short presentation and handed me the key to the city as a tribute. I was especially pleased when he gave a second key to Margie.

"Jan Shadburn, who was our county campaign coordinator, served as the master of ceremonies for the celebration. Frank Powledge, representing the local Caverns Golf Course, gave me a new set of golf clubs as a gift from the public. Bob Pforte, local car dealer and current president of the Jackson County Chamber of Commerce, gave a short presentation in which he noted that I had attained the highest political office achieved by any resident of Jackson County since Governor Milton during the Civil War.

"Margie and I were moved to tears as this tremendous homecoming took place. The outpouring of excitement, caring, and support for us was beyond comprehension. All we could do was say 'thank you!' over and over. It was an unforgettable homecoming.

"Bob and I were scheduled to meet with outgoing governor Rubin Askew in Tallahassee on Friday in order to review what was needed to accomplish an orderly transition. This would also give Bob and me an opportunity to discuss impending work related to forming our new administration organization. We wanted to solicit the very best talent possible for the implementation of the programs we had promised to enact.

"That evening, after Margie and I had finally reached the peace and quiet of our home, we reflected on what was happening. We were both excitedly anticipating the roles we were about to assume. It was astounding to realize that we were about to assume a leadership role in the direction of the great state of Florida. Our life-journey travels had risen to an unimaginable height, beyond anything we could have hoped for. The anticipation of what lay before us was thrilling. I prayed that my deep desire to help the people of Florida was about to become a reality."

Endnotes

1. Robert Shevin was born in Miami, Florida. He received his Bachelor's degree from the University of Florida in 1955, and his Juris Doctorate from the University of Miami in 1957. He also attended New York University School of Law. Shevin was elected to the Florida House of Representatives in 1964 and the Florida State Senate in 1966. He was elected attorney general in 1970 and re-elected in 1974. Shevin was an unsuccessful candidate for governor of Florida in 1978. He led the first round of the Democratic primary, but was defeated in the runoff by Bob Graham.

2. James A. Glisson (born January 6, 1939). Glisson was born in Jackson County, Florida. He attended Palmer College and earned a degree in chiropractic studies. He served in the Florida House of Representatives for the 33rd District from 1968 to 1972, as a Republican. He was elected to the State Senate in 1973 and served the 11th District until 1978. In 1976 he changed his party affiliation from Republican to Democratic.

3. Peninsula Motor Club is the Tampa-based affiliate of the American Automobile Association (AAA), and is an association of automobile dealers in the area. It promotes area tourism, business ethics in the automobile industry, and environmental awareness. The "Florida Explorer" publication the organization produces is widely read in the Tampa-St. Petersburg area.

4. Donald L. Tucker was a former speaker of the Florida House of Representatives and Special Ambassador for the United States to the Dominican Republic. Tucker earned his Juris Doctorate degree from the University of Florida in 1962. He served as speaker of the Florida House of Representatives from 1974 until 1978. The Tallahassee-Leon County Civic Center, home of the Florida State University Men's and Women's basketball teams, as well as other local teams, was renamed in honor of Tucker in 1977 and is now known as the Donald L. Tucker Center. (Source, Freebase.com)

5. Production Credit Association (PCA). A federal instrumentality created by Congress through the Farm Credit Act of 1933 to provide short- and intermediate-term credit to farmers, ranchers, and rural residents. This program was a Roosevelt-era Depression recovery effort to assist farmers in obtaining bank financing.

6. Jack Eckerd (May 16, 1913–May 19, 2004) was born in Wilmington, Delaware. The Eckerd chain, oldest of the major drugstore companies in the U.S., was founded by Jack's father, J. Milton Eckerd, in 1898. After serving as a pilot in World War II, Jack Eckerd started a phenomenal expansion of the chain by buying three stores in Florida in 1952. When Eckerd ultimately sold his shares in 1986, there were about 1,500 stores.

   In 1978 Eckerd defeated U.S. Representative Louis Frey Jr. of Winter Park to win the Republican gubernatorial nomination, but he lost in the fall to the Democrat Bob Graham of Miami.

7. Paula Hawkins (January 24, 1927–December 4, 2009). To date, she is the only woman elected to the U.S. Senate from Florida. In 1972 she became the first woman elected to statewide office in Florida by winning a seat on the Florida Public Service Commission. In 1978 she was the Republican candidate for lieutenant governor of Florida on the ticket headed by her former intraparty rival, Jack Eckerd. They lost to State Senator Bob Graham and State Representative Wayne Mixson. In 1980 she defeated Bill Gunter to win election to the United States Senate.

8. Hans Gearhart Tanzler Jr. was a Democratic Florida politician and judge. He served as mayor of Jacksonville, Florida, from 1967 to 1979. During his administration, the City of Jacksonville consolidated with Duval County, making him the last mayor of the old city government and the first mayor of a consolidated Jacksonville.

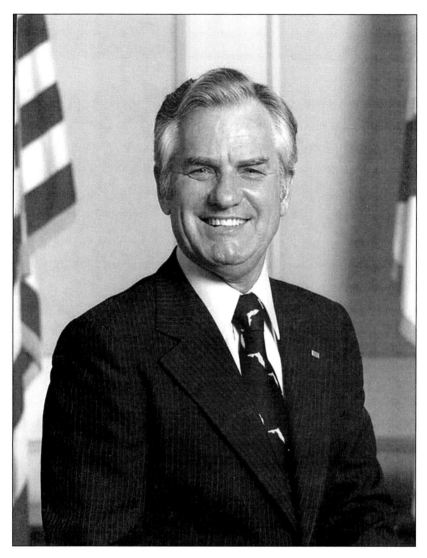

John Wayne Mixson served as Florida state representative, Florida lieutenant governor, and briefly as the 39th governor of Florida.

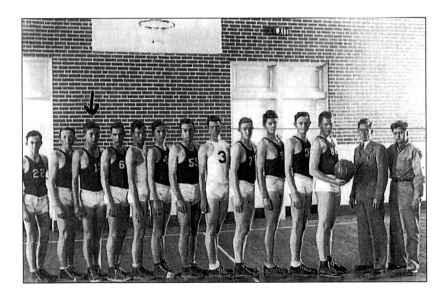

New Brockton High School Basketball Team, 1940. Arrow indicates
Wayne Mixson.

Wayne first met Margie when she was fourteen.

Wayne and Margie while he was home on leave.

New Brockton High School Senior Class of 1941. Arrow indicates Wayne
Mixson.

SENTRY OF THE SHIPPING LANE   WW II

Postcard from Wayne to his parents, 1943.

Seaman Wayne Mixson. Spring 1944.

War propaganda postcard sent home by Wayne.

Wayne with officer cadets at the University of Pennsylvania (he is sixth from left in middle row).

Wayne (top right) with Fiji Fraternity brothers while at Denison University, 1945.

Beautiful Margie Grace on the Florida State University campus, 1946.

December 27, 1947, in Graceville, Florida.

Florida House of Representatives, Wayne Mixson and Quillian Yancy. January 29, 1971.

Wayne Mixson takes his seat, 1967.

Wayne chats with Governor Reubin Askew.

Outgoing Governor Mixson talks with incoming Governor Martinez at the Governor's Mansion reception.

The entire Graham - Cracker Team!

Graham-Mixson work day

Gubernatorial candidate Sen. Robert Graham (right) confers with his runningmate, Rep. Wayne Mixson, during a break from a day-long sodding and house moving operation on S. Wynn St. in Marianna Saturday. The two men were among a group of 40 volunteers who took part in the proj t to prepare a Senior Citizens' Center for Ja son. Contians Other fficials taking part he

Raymond Bruner. The City of Marianna furnished the site on a 10-year lease, and the County Commission funded preparation of the land tract for a house donated by the First Methodist Church of Marianna. Graham and Mixson donated the sod. A spokesman for the Jackson County Senior Citizen's Council said the facility will be open five days per week. housing offices and recreation for senior

Two farmers discussing politics.

Graham and Cracker!

Wayne on the campaign trail.

Meet Governor Bob Graham!

Wayne becomes Lt. Governor Wayne Mixson.

Wayne and Margie with Florida Commissioner of Agriculture, Doyle Connors.

Wayne with Speaker of U.S. House of Representatives, Tip O'Neill; Senator Claude Pepper, and son.

Wayne poses with former Governor Buddy McKay and his wife, Anne.

Wayne talks with President Gerald Ford.

Wayne Mixson and Bob Graham meet with President Carter.

Wayne shakes hands with President Ronald Reagan.

Wayne poses for a picture with President George H. W. Bush.

Wayne visits with President George W. Bush.

Wayne with his longtime Jackson County friend, Amos Morris.

Wayne was also a pilot.

A favorite pastime was quail hunting.

The Florida Times-Union/Jacksonville Journal, Jacksonville, Sunday, January 4, 1987

— Associated Press

Wayne Mixson (center) takes the oath of office as governor of Florida from Supreme Court Justice Parker Lee McDonald (foreground) as Mixson's wife, Margie and former Gov. LeRoy Collins watch. Mixson's term as governor began yesterday and will end Tuesday. He jokingly offered to let his predecessor, who is now Sen. Bob Graham, serve as his lieutenant governor. Mixson also promised to carry out his duties "with dignity, with joy and a sense of fun."

Margie holds the family Bible as Wayne takes the oath of office for the governorship.

The Governor and his First Lady.

Wayne poses with a sign at the dedication ceremony making State Highway 73N in Jackson County the "Governor Mixson Highway."

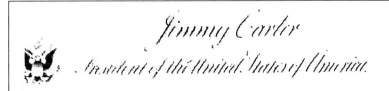

Jimmy Carter
President of the United States of America.

To His Excellency
Vice Admiral Alfredo Poveda Burbano,
President of the Supreme Council of
Government of Ecuador.

Excellency:

Desiring to give evidence of my appreciation of the cordial relations
existing between the United States of America and the Republic of Ecuador,
I have designated Wayne Mixson as my Representative, with the rank of
Special Ambassador, to attend the ceremonies incident to the inauguration
of His Excellency Dr. Jaime Roldos Aguilera as President of the Republic
of Ecuador.

I have entire confidence that Mr. Mixson will be acceptable to you
in the distinguished duty with which I have invested him.

I therefore ask that you receive my Representative favorably and
accept from him the renewed assurances of my high regard and of the
friendship which he bears of the Government and people of the United
States of America for you and the Government and people of the Republic
of Ecuador.

Very truly yours,

By the President:

Secretary of State.

Presidential Proclamation making Wayne Mixson the "Special Presidential Ambassador to Equador."

CHAPTER EIGHT

TRANSITION TIME IN TALLAHASSEE

With the hard-fought campaign finally over, Wayne and Margie had a few days of rest and reflection before they launched into working with Bob Graham to make preparations for taking charge of the executive branch of Florida's government in January. This meant making important decisions regarding filling critical appointments for the cabinet and key agency positions, and forming their administrative and advisory staff. Wayne was excited about the opportunities that were now open for him to accomplish some of the work that he felt was needed to help Florida and its citizens. Wayne describes his actions and emotions during this period.

"Margie immediately went back to work at Chipola College, saying that she had enjoyed the campaigning, but it was good to be back home. She announced that she planned to teach until spring, which would fulfill the requirements for her retirement. We were both flooded with a steady stream of phone calls from well-wishing friends and supporters.

"We discussed how great it was to see our pets again, which included our house dog, Stokeley, and my bird dog, Sue. They had been cared for by neighbors during our months of travel. We were grasping a short period of normalcy, but we knew a new lifestyle was just around the corner.

"Margie and I planned to lease an apartment in Tallahassee, while maintaining our home in Marianna. With the newly opened I-10 interstate, the travel time between Tallahassee and Marianna was shortened to one hour. That would help us maintain a presence in both locations.

"Shortly after the election an article appeared in the Enterprise, Alabama, newspaper, the *Enterprise Ledger*, heralding my election as the lieutenant governor of Florida. The article stressed the fact that I was born and raised at Mixson's Crossroads near New Brockton, in Coffee County. It also listed several of my relatives who still resided in Enterprise and in Coffee County. I was flattered by the acclaim, and very glad that my Alabama family received some notoriety.

"On Friday, November 10, Bob and I met with Governor Reubin Askew at his office in the state capitol. I had been to the executive offices on several occasions during the twelve years I worked in the legislature. I had usually been there to take part in some special media opportunity presentation, to discuss some issue or bill with someone, or to plead for assistance. It felt much different as I entered the suite this time.

"Reubin Askew was gracious and congratulatory as he greeted us. During the meeting we discussed ongoing programs and projects which involved Askew's administration and our new administration. We reviewed some of our immediate plans and solicited his opinions and input concerning them. We also discussed staff and administration personnel, existing and potential replacements. Bob and Reubin also discussed the transition required as occupancy of the governor's mansion changed. We attempted to develop a timetable to assure proper scheduling and arrangements.

"After the meeting, a short press conference was held. The governor expressed his anticipation of reentry into private life, thanked his supporters and staff for their wonderful work during his term of office, and in glowing terms expressed his satisfaction that he was being replaced by someone with the character, experience, and strengths of Bob Graham.

"Bob then expressed our deep gratitude to the thousands of people who had supported us during our long campaign. He described our immediate plans to finalize the staffing of our administration, and to immediately form the tax review committee which had been promised during the campaign. He also spent several minutes discussing the contributions that Margie and I had made to the victory. He stated that, without my huge impact in the Panhandle and middle Florida, we would not have won. I was embarrassed and gratified by his statements.

"We had decided to begin right away on implementing our plans as promised during our many campaign speeches. We wanted to leave a legacy which perpetuated and enhanced the 'Golden Years of Florida Politics,' which began in 1968 with the rewriting of Florida's constitution. Inauguration of the Graham-Mixson administration was set for January 2, 1979.

"Bob immediately assigned me the role of developing a new, efficient Department of Commerce within our administration which would work closely with local communities as they endeavored to attract appropriate industries to their areas.

"Programs and incentives would be developed to use as recruitment aids as industrial opportunities entered the scene. I welcomed the exciting opportunity to help form the mold that would shape industrial recruitment in Florida for many years. He also assigned me the task of forming the tax review commission and placing a two-year freeze on property taxes across the state while the review was being conducted.

"I began with my pet area of concern, bringing new industries and jobs to Florida. I still felt a desire to help those thousands of agricultural workers who had been displaced as new technologies were applied to the farming industries. I had witnessed their plight and had always felt a resolve to help them if an opportunity arose. To begin this process, we decided to conduct a series of regional meetings between community leaders, industry leaders in the area, and state officials. We would invite representatives from fifty to seventy companies in each area.

"The first of these meetings was held in Panama City on November 23, just three weeks after the election. We described some of the programs and concepts we were considering for implementation. We solicited feedback from the attendees. We tried to target desirable industrial sectors which we felt would fill community needs, protect the environment, create good jobs, and would find a Florida plant location advantageous.

"As initial target approaches, I felt we should build on Florida's strong agricultural base and entice more agricultural processing plants to the state. Second, I knew we had a great potential for development of a thriving export industry through improvement of our ports and making the needed contacts with importers throughout the world.

"Improvement of Florida's infrastructure, including roads and utilities, was another needed element which was discussed during these regional economic development meetings. Also, new state programs to assist locals in industrial site preparation for new industries were needed.

"We had numerous important programs which we wanted to get underway as soon as we took control of the executive branch. These included the tax review commission, improving strained relations between state government and local governments, property tax relief to assist home ownership, which included a two-year freeze on property tax increases, and a meaningful economic development program to create needed jobs in Florida.

"As input from the regional economic leadership meetings began to form, I began working on an implementation plan for our economic development goals. This involved the rebuilding of the state's Department of Commerce, which I would initially be managing. I realized that we had to convert the government's historical total focus on tourism into a broader, more effective, pro-business attitude. This would include measures to entice states, developing systems which would maximize coordination between the state and local industries, to consider Florida locations, incentives to compete effectively with neighboring economic development efforts, reduction of restrictive rules and regulations which inhibit economic development, speeding and simplification of the permitting processes, and use of local tax incentives.

"Internally, we were going to have to retrain, replace, and reeducate the state's bureaucracy in order to develop the necessary climate for the creation of a new business environment in Florida. Everyone in state government had to realize we were serious in this effort."

Margie, Back in the Classroom

Wayne pauses for a moment and begins to tell of Margie's experiences during this period. "While Bob and I were working feverishly at forming our administration and putting the beginnings of our new programs into place, Margie had returned to the Chipola College campus and her familiar classroom environment. Initially she was treated as a campus celebrity, with all of her old friends giving her congratulations and asking a multitude of questions about the campaigning.

"In a great article which was written in the school paper they portrayed an interview with Margie. The story noted that she had embarked from Marianna in a tattered old white and green Winnebago as a teacher and farmer's wife, and had triumphantly returned in a private jet as the wife of the lieutenant governor.

"It was all like a fantastic adventure with a fairy tale ending," Margie explained. "At first I was shy and hesitant about getting very involved, but after a while I was swept into the effort and became a part of it all. I particularly enjoyed meeting so many new, wonderful people. They were there everywhere we went, doing anything they could to help us. Also, I visited almost every one of the sixty-seven counties in Florida and saw firsthand the tremendous beauty and geographic diversity of our state."

"Then she described what our life had been like during the campaign. She related how we were scheduled each week out of our Tampa campaign headquarters. We would receive a printed weekly schedule which included a very detailed time schedule for each day. For example, it would begin:

6:00 Awake and Dress
6:30 Breakfast
7:30 Travel to ....

'All you had to do every day was follow the schedule. It was like being a robot since you made few personal decisions. Seriously, it all was fun and tremendously educational,' Margie said.

"Margie also revealed some of the more humorous incidents which had occurred. She constantly wore a large green and white Graham-Mixson badge. At one function the host read the badge and then introduced her to the crowd as 'Mrs. Graham Mixson.'

"On another occasion she was having a conversation with a community leader who knew Bob Graham quite well. He was expounding on how extraordinarily intelligent Bob Graham was. 'In fact, I fear that if the public knew how smart Bob really was, that he might lose votes because voters might not want to vote for an overly brilliant man.' Then he went on to say, 'That is why it is so good that he has Wayne Mixson on the ticket with him to provide a balance!'

"The article then went on to say that Graham was fortunate that he had chosen me as his running mate, since we won so decidedly in North Florida and had won in South Florida counties by a much smaller margin.

"Margie related how, during the run-off campaign against Shevin, we had not really thought we would win. She described how we carefully worked on words to use in a concession speech that would show we were losing gracefully. Then after we won the Democratic nomination, she began to believe that 'we might just win this thing!'

"She concluded the interview by describing what she termed as the 'most thrilling moments of the campaign,' as we landed in Marianna and were greeted by the large, enthusiastic crowd of friends and supporters. The story concluded with a note that Margie planned to finish the term at Chipola and then retire from teaching to work with me in Tallahassee.

"During the inauguration planning Margie and I decided that for the swearing-in we would use an old family Bible which had been given to me by my mother. Margie would hold the Bible as I placed my right hand upon it and repeated the required oath of office. I was not scheduled to make an address at the inauguration, since both outgoing Governor Askew and incoming Governor Graham were speaking."

Work and Worries from the Start

During the two-month period between the election and the inauguration there was much important work to accomplish in forming the new administration, scheduling, and determining priorities. However, Wayne was also still the representative for his district, and this legislative responsibility could not be ignored. In fact, that workload seemed to be increasing.

Wayne describes how difficult this period was for him. "On top of the existing workload, suddenly the large paper mill in Bay County which was owned by International Paper Company announced that it was closing their facility, which would cause the Panama City area to lose around 900 much-needed jobs. I began working feverishly to find another company that might be interested in purchasing the plant to prevent the closure. The reason for the decision to close was related to the fact that the equipment in the facility was all old technology.

"I tried to dispel statements that the environmental regulations had contributed to the decision. I explained that it was forced compliance with new federal EPA regulations which had created the problem. In order to bring their emissions into compliance with the newest requirements, the company would be forced to spend $17,000,000 on control systems. The total cost of modernizing the plant would approach $100,000,000. I proclaimed that the state would provide 'total assistance' in an effort to save the business.

"Another major time-consuming project which was before us was the fact that the biennial budget was due for presentation in mid-February. Budget workshops were already underway in the legislature and were occupying much of my time. I had to be sure the Department of Commerce was well funded in the new budget if we were going to be able to begin the economic development programs we had planned.

"During all of this I had to make a trip to New York City to meet with the top executives of several industrial prospects with whom we had begun discussing Florida locations. I also met with top executives of Pan American Airlines, which we had learned was considering merging with financially troubled Florida-based National Airlines. The merger would cause Florida to lose thousands of jobs. When I returned to Florida, I arranged a meeting with Miami-based Eastern Air Lines, which was also considering a merger with National.

"The work pace was brutal. For instance, even on Inauguration Day I was scheduled with over thirty appointments. Throw in media interviews and unscheduled visitors and you have the full picture of the fervor which was suddenly underway. Remarkably, I had not even taken over the lieutenant governor's job yet. 'We're paddling from behind!' I pleaded. After the inauguration we began to announce the filling of key staff positions and things soon began to normalize—somewhat.

"During this time, I was living in a Tallahassee hotel during the week, and spending weekends with Margie in Marianna. Margie and I planned to buy a townhouse in Tallahassee when she finished her school term in the spring. On the farm the planting season was about to begin, yearling cows were grazing, and there was farm work to be done. I was lucky to be able to spend a few hours out of a week on the farm, but thankfully I had a great crew employed to manage the farming operation."

The Inauguration

Tuesday, January 2, 1979, dawned: a chilly, blustery day as a fast-moving front swept through the area. By mid-morning temperatures hovered at 31 degrees with a brisk 35-mile-per-hour gusting wind from the north. It was no day for an outside ceremony. It was an unforgettable day for Wayne and Margie.

"The inauguration process in Florida is closely controlled by tradition. Starting time for our inaugural event was 11:00 a.m. outside on the capitol lawn. The ceremony involves an impressive mixture of politics, religion, military, music, and more politics. It was unbelievable that there were twenty-three committees involved in the planning and coordination of the ceremonies. They covered everything from seating to flower arrangements.

"The planned agenda allowed for local religious leaders to lead prayers at appropriate points during the ceremonies. A talented young singer was to sing the state song, "Old Folks at Home," and as a grand finale there was to be a nineteen-gun salute which would signal every church in Tallahassee to begin a bell-ringing serenade of the city.

"Four thousand folding chairs were arranged in Waller Park on the west side of the capitol building, where the speaking platform was waiting. Of these seats, approximately eight hundred were reserved for families of the honorees, campaign staff, media, and other special dignitaries.

"I regretted that so many people, including our families and many friends, were going to have to endure these elements while they attended our inauguration. I realized that the conditions were going to make the ceremonies as brisk and brief as possible. There would be no long, extemporaneous speeches and few lingering post-event conversations. Before the day was over it would even spray a few fast-flying snowflakes. It was cold!"

The day's activities began with a special 8:30 morning prayer service which was held at Florida A&M. The day ended with the inaugural ball which was held at Florida State's Tully Gym. The dignitaries who were to be involved in the ceremonies were seated on the platform on schedule. Most of them were clad in winter coats and still struggling to stay warm.

Wayne describes the ceremony, "Because of the cold, Bob was sworn in as Florida's 38th governor sixteen minutes before the traditional high noon reciting of the oath of office, as the pace of the preceding ceremonies had been sped through in less than the initially allotted times. Former governor Leroy Collins, who was the master of ceremonies, excused the Florida State marching band from playing scheduled tunes. Then he said in a shivering voice, 'I realize that the appointed time of noon has not yet arrived, but let's all pretend that it is here and proceed with the oath.' There was no opposition to his suggested course of action.

"Governor Askew delivered his farewell remarks. 'I thank the Lord for sustaining us during these eight years of service. I leave today with a deep sense of satisfaction as a difficult and demanding stewardship comes to an end. When I took office eight years ago, I said on my inauguration day that I would make some errors, and I am sure that I have. But I also pledged that they would not be errors of nonconcern or of nonaction. I pray that I have been true to that pledge.'

"Then he praised his staff and those who had assisted his administration. 'I feel we have accomplished much, but those judgments are for others . . . and for history.' He continued with comments on the uncertainty of the future and our reliance on Florida's wonderful natural heritage. He described how Florida is a 'bridge' between the continents of South America and North America, and how Florida is a 'crossroads' of tourism and commerce. 'Florida is on the cutting edge of an international tomorrow,' he said. 'I leave knowing that state government in Florida will be in good and capable hands. I rejoice that my successor is as well qualified and knowledgeable as he is. His administration begins on a high note at a time of great promise. I know that every Floridan of good will prays for his strength and wisdom as he assumes leadership of our great state,' Governor Askew concluded.

"Following the governor's remarks, 'Suwanee River' was sung by Julianne Roland. Then oaths of office were administered to Commissioner of Education Ralph Turlington, Commissioner of Agriculture Doyle Connor, State Treasurer Bill Gunter, Comptroller Gerald Lewis, Attorney General Jim Smith, and Secretary of State George Firestone. It was the next ceremony and oath which made me the new lieutenant governor. It was a thrilling moment for Margie and me. I was sworn in with my beloved Margie standing at my side holding our family Bible. Then Governor-elect Bob Graham took center stage.

"Bob Graham rose to take his oath of office. Chief Justice Arthur England Jr. administered the traditional oath to the incoming governor. After his oath, Bob's family pastor, the Reverend Dr. Harold Youngblood, administered a sincerely worded prayer.

"Next, outgoing secretary of state, J. J. McCrary, delivered the Great Seal of Florida to Governor Askew who, as prescribed by tradition, passed the state emblem to Bob Graham, thus officially transferring the powers of the office. At that time the nineteen-gun salute began.

"The new governor began his remarks. In his short inaugural address, Bob delivered his message of hope and progress. He began 'I stand here today on this timeless hill before two capitol buildings. One is the symbol of the Florida that was, and the other is the symbol of the Florida that can be. Our historic capitol symbolizes the first dreams of a united Florida. It reminds us of the hopes and aspirations of our predecessors.

"'Our gleaming new capitol symbolizes our own dreams. It reminds us of the challenging future we share in working for a better Florida. As we make a new beginning for Florida, we must be hopeful for our future and mindful of our past. For the past and the future are intertwined with the present.' He went on to describe how, in 1823, Dr. William Simmons had traveled westward from St. Augustine, while John Lee Williams traveled eastward from Pensacola. The two men met at St. Marks and then moved northward, seeking a site which would become Florida's capitol. Bob related how they finally arrived at the very hill we were presently occupying. They were amazed at the prevailing beauty of the trees, plants, and abundant wildlife, and thus agreed this was to be the site.

"Graham continued, 'We are the heirs to the Florida which flourished so many years ago. We are the beneficiaries of all the dreamers of other days. We are the inheritors of all the white sands on the beaches, the mysteries of the Everglades, the secrets of the grassy savannahs, and the vast silence of the forest.' He spoke for only twenty-three minutes. It was a stirring, meaningful speech. I wished that more people could have been there to hear him deliver it.

"I regretted that the bone-chilling cold on our inauguration day had reduced the number of attendees from an expected 15,000 to about 3,000 of the most loyal and hardy. We had wanted it to be a festive, fun affair, 'The People's Inauguration,' but Mother Nature had taken control. The bitter cold created some unusual apparel to appear at our ceremony. For instance, Senate President Gerald Lewis of Palm Beach was sitting on the speakers' platform wearing a huge set of Micky Mouse earmuffs. Agricultural Commissioner Doyle Conner wanted to go find some thermal long john underwear to put on. One of our supporters who was there commented, 'When I decided to go, I told someone that I would freeze to death before I would miss the inauguration. I almost did!'

"During the inaugural parade, Bob quipped, 'I guess it is only appropriate that on the day the first South Florida governor is sworn in, it would be snowing in Tallahassee.' He also noted that he felt a satisfied, 'inner warmth' that was countering the weather.

"That evening the inaugural ball was held at the Tallahassee Civic Center and our supporters, friends, and staff were finally able to celebrate. For me, the evening was a blur of hugs, handshakes, and introductions, occasionally fortified by a morsel of food, and a moment of rest. The music was continuous, with two or three separate entertainment groups playing. Margie and I have never been party animals, although we do enjoy being around people. The ball was a whirlwind, and we had a good time.

"That evening, when we finally were preparing to turn out the light and go to sleep, Margie and I embraced and talked. We both found it hard to realize that we were about to assume the second highest leadership role in the state of Florida. I praised Margie for the supportive role she had played throughout the long campaign. She stated that she felt assurance that Bob Graham and I would do much to help move Florida forward during our term. As I turned out the light, my mind was spinning with details and plans to get our programs underway."

CHAPTER NINE

LIEUTENANT GOVERNOR WAYNE MIXSON

1978–1986

With the launching of the Graham-Mixson administration, Florida was entering a new era of managed growth. Destined to serve as a two-term administration, they would leave a legacy of having brought Florida to the forefront in industrial recruitment, jobs creation, international commerce, environmental awareness, advancements in education, infrastructure improvements, urban development, tax reforms, government efficiencies, and social diversity. After the inauguration, Governor Bob Graham and Lt. Governor Wayne Mixson soon moved into their new offices in the executive suite of the state capitol. These uniquely teamed former legislators, one a liberal-leaning, urban-minded Democrat and the other a conservative-leaning, rural-oriented Democrat, had developed a combined platform that held great promise for the citizens of Florida. They eagerly began the task of fulfilling their campaign promises.

Wayne begins, "On that first day it felt good to sit behind the desk of the lieutenant governor of Florida in the large, well-appointed office which was provided for the second-highest political office in the state. I felt I was ready for the tasks which had been assigned to me and was ready to get to work. Bob and I had agreed that I would be an active part of our administration and would not be relegated to being a stand-in for the governor, attending funerals and political events on his behalf. I was to also function as the head official of the Florida Department of Commerce, the liaison between the county governments and the state government, and eventually to also serve as the liaison between the Graham administration and the legislature. Also, my initial task was to chair several regional meetings of a special tax revision commission. Another top priority activity was participation in the staffing of a new, revitalized Department of Commerce which I would direct. On that first day I began action on these projects."

Tax Revision Commission

During their first term Wayne chaired the tax revision commission as appointed by the governor. The goals of this commission were to make Florida's taxes fair, adequate, and supportive of the administration's overall goals. These goals included creating more and better jobs by improving the business climate, increasing home ownership, protecting the environment, funding education, and improving transportation and other essential services.

After conducting a series of regional meetings, the tax commission used the information which had been accumulated to form five constitutional amendments as their recommendations. These were known as "Five for Florida's Future." The amendments passed both houses of the legislature with 75 percent support, thus enabling the commission to offer them to the voters in the next election. Next, they were approved overwhelmingly by Florida's voters. The legislature then passed implementing legislation. This tax-related legislation significantly changed several aspects of state taxation in Florida. Most of these changes have endured the passage of time. This body of legislation was a very significant step forward for Florida and is a part of the legacy of the Graham-Mixson administration.

Wayne describes the process, "These regional meetings of the tax commission were attended by community leaders from the area, top industrial representatives, businessmen, industrial development specialists, and key politicians. We discussed local needs, property taxation policies, funding of education, social programs, wages for government workers, law enforcement needs, environmental issues, potential incentives for enlisting new industries to locate plants in Florida, coordination between local industrial recruitment efforts and the Department of Commerce, and most of all, sources of funding. I found that there was a great diversity of opinions among the participants regarding spending, levels of services, and funding sources. The input which came from these meetings, which were held in five cities around the state, was invaluable.

"We set out immediately to communicate these changes to the business world in Florida, nationwide, and worldwide. As a result, national ranking agencies upped Florida from a rating in the thirties to the number one business climate in the nation. The marketing personnel in the Florida Department of Commerce were increased and set out to find new and higher paying jobs. Offices were established in Germany to serve Europe and in Japan to serve the Far East, and regional offices were established in the United States.

"Wearing the 'Florida Number One' pins and the 'E' award button presented to Florida by President Reagan at ceremonies in the oval office, Florida agents were well received in corporate offices everywhere. Florida's business and tourism grew rapidly. 'People like to work where they like to live,' was a slogan, and 10,000 of them were moving to Florida every day.

"Under my leadership, the Department of Commerce assisted in the location or expansion of more than 600 businesses in Florida, leading the nation in the number of new jobs created. One of the fastest-growing elements of Florida's economy was the international sector, which increased foreign trade, banking, and investments. Florida also became the third-largest state in motion picture and television production, creating thousands of jobs.

"Florida enjoyed growth in the high tech and manufacturing industries during the 1980s. Hundreds of thousands of high-paying jobs were created by such companies as Motorola, IBM, Harris, United Technologies, and Sony. Over 100 foreign Edge Act banks established offices or agencies in Florida to serve the rapidly growing foreign trade with Florida, and through Florida to Central and South America.

"Combined with Florida's robust tourism, construction, agriculture, finance, and service industries, Florida employed a more varied and balanced economy than it had previously. Florida weathered the recession of the early 1980s much better than most states as a result of our growing economy, which provided tax revenues and enabled the state to continue improvements in education, transportation, and essential services. By the time our second term ended, Florida was recognized as a very probusiness state, a great place to expand and work, and our diverse economy was one of the best in any state. I take great pride in what we accomplished, and the positive impact it had on thousands of needy workers."

"Sweet Home Alabama!"

Wayne and Margie both take great pride in their families' lineage. Their ancestries are generously punctuated with outstanding individuals who took an active part in their communities and the governments of their era. During the early days of settlement of the South during the 1800s, Wayne's ancestors played important roles in south Alabama, while Margie's ancestors were doing similar service a few miles farther south, in Florida. The Jackson County town of Graceville was named after her great-grandfather. When Wayne was elected lieutenant governor of Florida, Alabama took note.

Wayne explains, "They say that the place where you grow up and attend school is the place which you will always identify as home. Those formative years and the wonderful experiences of youth remain forever ingrained within your soul. For me, the south Alabama farm at Mixson's Corner will always be home. I love Jackson County, Florida, and spent most of my life living in that wonderful locale, but Alabama will always hold a special place for me.

"Unfortunately, the old adage, 'You can't go back home,' is true, if you attempt to move back to your home to recoup your youth once you leave. However, I did get to return to my Alabama roots for one day. It was a day I will never forget. It was the day proclaimed by the Alabama legislature and Alabama Governor Fob James as 'Wayne Mixson Day.' The idea was spawned by Alabama Lieutenant Governor George McMillan, after we met and discussed my Alabama heritage during a lieutenant governors' conference. After he returned home, he instigated the movement to create the recognition of me and my ancestors.

"Margie and I were flown to Montgomery from Tallahassee in an Alabama state aircraft which was sent to pick us up. The day began with a special reception in our honor which was held at the Capital City Club in Montgomery. At that event Margie and I were both presented plaques and I was given a letter of recognition from the governor. They were presented to us by Lieutenant Governor McMillan. I stood behind the head table, thanked everyone for attending, and recognized our family and friends who were there. I then related the story of how my father and I had traveled from our farm to Montgomery to sell syrup and hams. I also recalled how I took my first airplane ride on one trip to Montgomery, and it had cost us three buckets of syrup. I had difficulty holding back tears as I tried to explain how much this special recognition meant to me.

"Then the ceremonies continued at the Alabama State Capitol. First, we went to the House chamber where I was honored to be presented to the Alabama House of Representatives by the House speaker. It was very emotional for me to be standing in the same location that my great-grandfather had stood when he served as a member of the Alabama House of Representatives.

"Then we moved to the Senate chamber. I was ushered into the chamber and taken to the podium where Lt. Governor McMillan introduced me to the Senate membership. I was overwhelmed as the entire body stood and applauded on my behalf. The balconies were filled with my family members, friends, and youngsters from area Alabama schools. McMillan introduced me by giving a brief background, and then turned the microphone over to me.

"Once again, I related my story about coming to Montgomery to sell syrup and hams when I was a boy. I also told of my great-grandfather's role as a state representative. I explained that in 1854 he was part of a commission that went to Tallahassee to try for the annexation of Northwest Florida into Alabama. There was another attempt for annexation years later and my uncle, John Simmons, headed the commission. Both attempts failed.

"I described the level of mutual cooperation that existed between Alabama and Florida in those days, and how we needed to advance the same spirit today. Then McMillan introduced Margie and invited everyone to a special reception in our honor.

"On the way to the reception, I was given a book titled *The Role of the Senate in Alabama History*, by the Secretary of the Senate, McDowell Lee. We immediately opened the book and quickly found references to several of my ancestors. It was a very meaningful gift which I prize very highly.

"The reception was well attended, and Lt. Governor McMillan stood beside Margie and me and introduced almost everyone there to us, giving their title and background. After the reception we were interviewed by the local media, and I once again tried to express our gratitude and what an emotional occasion it was for me. Finally we were returned to Tallahassee, and one of the most memorable days of my life came to an end.

"I love Florida, and Jackson County is my cherished home, but I will always save a little room for my childhood memories in Sweet Home Alabama."

Creating Jobs—The Florida Department of Commerce

Prior administrations had traditionally focused on promoting and developing tourism to provide job growth and a boost to the economy of Florida. As a result, the Florida Department of Commerce had become an underfunded, understaffed, ineffective effort for recruitment of new industries and jobs in Florida. This approach had a positive impact on Central and South Florida, but did little to help boost the economies in the rest of the state. Wayne was determined to correct this situation.

Wayne begins, "Creating jobs for those migrating from the farms in my district and other farming areas because of mechanization and consolidation on the farms, and creating better jobs for the underemployed people in Florida, became the number one priority for me during my political career. I was motivated by a deep, ingrained personal desire to bring many new jobs to Florida and thus provide a better standard of living for those thousands of rural farm laborers who had been displaced as modern technologies were introduced to the farming industries. It was going to be a tough task, but I knew it was achievable. The opportunity to significantly further this cause was afforded in the governor's office, when I teamed up with Bob Graham and we won the election. Acting as business ambassador for Florida to the U.S. and major business centers throughout the world provided a fruitful opportunity to bring new jobs to our state.

"One of the prime goals of the Graham-Mixson administration was to broaden Florida's economy through diversification and higher wages. Additional goals were to provide jobs for Florida's young people, who often left Florida for better opportunities, and to establish a growing tax base to serve a rapidly growing population. The plan was for Florida to grow a tax base, rather than taxing the existing limited base.

"The task of staffing the new Florida Department of Commerce with the best industrial recruitment talents available was not easy. We brought in Sidney Levin, who had been the president of the Greater Miami Chamber of Commerce, to serve as director of the Florida Department of Commerce. After much effort we finally assembled a very capable group of industrial recruitment specialists and were ready to begin the job of bringing new jobs to Florida.

"One element of industrial recruitment which we had to immediately address was changing the prevailing image of the state as a great place to visit and play, but not as a good place to locate and start a new business or plant. We had to develop a reputation for being a pro-industry state. Florida had a lot to offer, but we were in direct competition with neighboring states throughout the South. I felt that Florida was ideally positioned to become a major participant in the nation's growing export-import activities, especially in the Caribbean, South America, and Europe.

"Although industrial development initiatives were an area of focus for the Department of Commerce as we launched our new pro-industry programs, tourism remained a major element of Florida's economy. We began an aggressive advertising program directed at increasing tourism in Florida, nationally and internationally. The advertising was focused on Canada, the Northeast, Midwest, and South. From our efforts, we realized a ten percent increase in tourism in 1986, involving over thirty-five million visitors to the state. The tourism rate rose steadily throughout the eight years Bob and I were in charge of the Florida Department of Commerce and Tourism."

Creating Jobs—Probusiness Legislation

"I knew that the first step in creating a meaningful climate within Florida for soliciting new industrial investments in the state was to pass legislation which would facilitate creation of incentives for prospective industries which were attractive and competitive with what our neighboring states were offering.

"A second step which was needed was the elimination of the tax levied on inventories which was paid by industries on the products they held in stock. This tax required difficult recordkeeping for some types of businesses and did not yield very much revenue for the state. We needed to abolish this tax.

"The results of the work completed by the tax revision commission created five constitutional amendments which were recommended for action by the legislature. These were given the title 'Five for Florida's Future,' and were passed overwhelmingly by the legislature and then the voters of Florida. Among these were: (1) A provision which established the homestead exemption for homeowners at a level of $25,000, (2) Provision for exemption from taxation for household improvements which involved adding solar equipment, (3) Authorization for state issuance of tax-free bonds for low interest loans for housing and related facilities for low and middle income families, (4) Authorization for counties and municipalities to issue industrial development exemptions for property taxes for specified periods up to ten years, (5) Abolishing the existing inventory tax which was levied against products held in stock for future sale by businesses. This was a tax which charged a manufacturer one percent on the value of raw materials in stock, and ten percent on finished goods inventories.

"Among the most important pieces of probusiness legislation which was needed in Florida was legislation enabling local county and municipal governments to pass limited exemptions from local property taxation for companies willing to locate in the community by making investments in new job-producing plants.

"Other legislation which was recommended included bills which provided that agricultural lands could be assessed at value based on current usage, and that tangible properties held for sale such as stocks, crops, or livestock could be assessed at a percentage of their market value. By the end of the first session in 1981, we had most of this needed legislation and required constitutional amendments approved. This helped tremendously as we launched our industrial recruitment programs."

Creating Jobs—Trade Missions

"During our first term, at the Mayor's Economic Development Council meeting, I made a pledge that during the next four years we would bring at least 175,000 new jobs to Florida."

Throughout his time as lieutenant governor, Wayne was engaged heavily with Department of Commerce activities. He led many trade missions to industrial centers and government capitals around the world. He would assemble a contingent of Florida business and government leaders to accompany him as they targeted foreign companies that were interested in enhancing their trade activities with Florida and the United States. Leading these missions occupied much of Wayne's time and attention. Wayne discusses the importance of the trade missions.

"These trade missions were a major component of our effort to entice new industrial investments within Florida. The missions were primarily designed to increase Florida's participation in international commerce, since our state is ideally situated for international trade with the Caribbean, South America, Asia, and Europe. By the end of our second term, we had engaged in over sixty trade missions.

"I recall several memorable missions to Japan. Most of our missions included an involvement with the American Embassy. I always tried to make my first appointment in a country with the U.S. ambassador for briefings regarding political and business activities in the nation we were visiting. This procedure always made me well prepared to deal with the local political and economic issues.

"From my years of official foreign travel, and dozens of such meetings with members of the diplomatic corps, I developed a deep respect for their capabilities, intelligence, patriotism, and dedication to the United States. After each trip I always sent a letter to the secretary of state, providing my assessment of contacts in every country we had visited. The ambassador in Japan at the time of our visit was Mike Mansfield. He was a former U.S. senator from Montana who served as ambassador in Japan under several U.S. presidents, and none had wanted him to retire.

"In my opinion, few of our ambassadors had the political skills and courtly manners of Mike Mansfield. His plans, when he eventually did retire, were to build a retirement home in Boca Grande, Florida. He and I developed a good friendship as a result of several meetings we enjoyed during my trips to Japan.

"On several occasions, on my first morning in Japan the ambassador would send his limousine to the Imperial Hotel to pick me up for breakfast at the embassy residence with him and his wife, Maureen. On one of the occasions when I was enjoying breakfast with the ambassador and his wife, I had made arrangements with the Florida citrus commission to have two crates of Florida oranges and grapefruit delivered to their residence while we were eating. It was a big surprise for them, and they seemed to appreciate the gifts. While giving me a tour of the house, the ambassador picked up a telephone from his desk and said, 'This is the phone on which General McArthur received his invitation to retire from his command in Korea.' I was impressed by the historical significance of the residence."

Some of the missions which Wayne organized through the Department of Commerce were designed to promote international trade with a specific geographic area of Florida, such as Miami, the Tampa Bay Area, the Gulf Coast, or other areas. Some trade missions were organized to create introductions between a specific U.S. industry group and a similar group in targeted foreign countries. Examples of this were the aircraft industry, aerospace, and agriculture. Missions might be focused on increasing usage of Florida's international ports.

Wayne continues, "In April of 1983 I led a Tampa Bay Area task force of about 100 members, representing six counties around the Bay area, on an international trade mission to Britain and Germany. The defined objective of this trip was to accomplish the 'internationalism of the Tampa Bay area.' This was a three-pronged attack into Europe, aimed at opening up export opportunities, encouraging foreign investments, and boosting foreign tourism in Florida.

"The mission chairman was Park Wright III,[1] a member of the powerful Lykes family holdings. The itinerary for the trip included stops in London, Glasgow, Frankfort, and Stuttgart.

"Upon arrival in London, the mission first met with the U.S. ambassador, then held business appointments the rest of the day. That evening they held a reception for the London business community at the American Embassy. The next day, at the London Chamber, the group conducted an informative seminar about the Tampa Bay Area. That evening, another reception was held for the local business community. Then the mission left London for Glasgow, and two days of appointments with local business leaders. In Germany we visited a very famous winery at Schloss Vollrads,[2] hosted by my good friend, Grof Ereneim Matuschma. That night I hosted a dinner at Grafenhausen with many of the leading businessmen in the area as guests.

"The next morning we departed Frankfort by automobile, heading for Stuttgart. Our chairman, Park Wright, had some unpleasant memories related to Stuttgart, dating back to 1944 and World War II. His B-17 was shot down near the city, and he was forced to bail out of the aircraft. Unfortunately, his parachute became entangled in a tree on a nearby farm, leaving him dangling and helpless. He was soon captured by local farmers who paraded him about the town as a trophy captive. Park still felt some bitterness over the experience.

"I was aware of Park's experience, so I assured him that we held a 'first class' reception in Stuttgart. Our first business visit was with Manfred Rommel, son of the famed German field marshal, Erwin Rommel, who was known as the Desert Fox in the German Army. After a very friendly reception with dignitaries, press, and photographers, Park was to be welcomed with another, even grander, reception by the provencal minister, Luther Speight. This, of course, caught the eye of the community, and made the mission a spectacular success. Park was immensely pleased and forgot his resentment of the treatment he had experienced during the war."

Overall, this trade mission was very successful. There is no way to calculate the total impact of the vast expansion in trade for the Tampa Bay area that resulted from this trip. Several companies realized fruitful trade contracts from introductions generated by the mission. Many of these are still in effect today. Trade missions such as this usually result in great gains in commerce and cultural exchange. The Tampa Bay area is still reaping compounded returns from this Mixson-led trade mission in 1983.

Wayne describes another of the many trade missions he led to develop foreign markets for Florida's business communities. "This time it was a group comprised of Miami and South Florida based businessmen, politicians, and media, and the targeted country was Italy. We left the Miami airport on a direct flight to Rome.

"Soon after our arrival we assembled for an informative meeting with the U.S. ambassador to Italy, Maxwell Rabb.[3] Later that evening the ambassador hosted a reception for our group at the embassy. After his initial introduction, we were ready for the city and its business community.

"The next day, as usual on such trips, the first item on our schedule was an early morning meeting with the mayor of Rome, Walter Veltroni. In order to give us a proper welcome, and to demonstrate the atmosphere of this grand, historic city, he held his welcome greeting from the marble steps of his office. As we listened to his remarks, all the glory that was Rome—at least the visible evidence of his glorious city—lay before us with its massive rivers and architectural wonders. None of us could fail to experience awe and appreciation of this grandiose setting.

"I expressed our thanks to the mayor for his hospitality, and for entertaining us so spectacularly, but I could not help inquiring, 'Mr. Mayor, how can you reconcile all of this glory, and your pride, with your title as the Communist Mayor of Rome? All of this archeology, artistic work in buildings, in sculptures, in artwork in the Sistine Chapel, and many other sites to be seen and left for you and the world by Christian artists and sponsors, does not seem to be the work of godless Communists, does it?'

"The Miami newsmen traveling with our group later remarked about my 'rude' question. But the mayor had apparently pondered this question many times in the past, and he skillfully reminded me that Euro-communism was not the same as the type of Communism imagined by Westerners. I was fortunate to get away from the occasion on friendly terms, thanks to the political skills of the Communist Mayor of Rome.

"As our mission moved to other Italian cities I realized that he was not alone. Several of the main cities of Italy also had Communist officials. Before I left I apologized to Ambassador Rabb, explaining that my curiosity had made me do it. He assured me that no damage had been caused by my inquiry. From this experience I learned that the world goes on, and we have to get accustomed to its truths and changes."

In 1986 Wayne led another trade mission, this time to China. He tells the story: "The mission to China was sponsored by the U.S. Department of Commerce and included about twenty people. The mission was primarily focused on aircraft supplies, engines, repairs, and airport loading ramps, called 'bridges.' At the time China's rapid industrial development was providing a very favorable foreign exchange rate, and a priority in their spending was in transportation facilities. Chinese air transport service from Florida could be expanded in a short time, and it was an area of need in China as industry there was growing rapidly.

"On this mission we visited two cities, Beijing and Shanghai. In Beijing we were formally entertained, and our industrial representatives were allowed to describe their products and services to the Minister of Aviation and his aviation professionals. Later, the same presentations we made in Beijing were also made in Shanghai.

"Our first workday in Beijing was very fruitful, as many contracts were signed by a variety of our members for aircraft parts, loading ramps for airports, and other aviation-related products. Also, the Orlando Helicopter Company was able to find markets for their older, small, used helicopters. These were to be used by the Chinese as air ambulances, and as crop dusters for farmers. They were old, gasoline-type helicopters and could be operated and maintained economically in China's rural areas. The largest sale for the mission group was for $200 million worth of aircraft jet engines. These engines were to be used, as they are in many U.S. cities, as backup or auxiliary engines for generating electricity at maximum demand times, or in emergencies.

"On about the third day in Beijing they hosted a banquet honoring the assistant secretary of the U.S. Department of Commerce and me in the Great Hall of the People.[4] We all enjoyed the colorful presentation at the banquet and I learned to love authentic Chinese food.

"One of the most exciting personal experiences for me was when I had the opportunity to stay at the Jin Jiang Hotel[5] in Shanghai. It is a very old and historic hotel, and has hosted many U.S. dignitaries. Because I was the only visitor they had at the time with any political title, they invited me to occupy the presidential suite at no extra cost. Later they told me that I had slept in the same bed used by Presidents Ronald Reagan and Jimmy Carter. The decor of the hotel was very oriental and beautiful. I remind the reader that my occupancy of this wonderful suite was at their suggestion and at the standard room rate. They seemed to get as much pleasure in hosting us as we did in experiencing their grandeur.

"The overall mission to China was very successful. A few months later a delegation of about twenty people came to the U.S. from China to accomplish a contract signing. I attended the event, which was held in an Orlando Chinese restaurant."

Wayne describes another trip to Asia, "One year, while I was lieutenant governor, I attended a trade conference in Taipei,[6] Taiwan. I participated in several seminars featuring U.S. officials, U.S. governors, trade association leaders, and high-level officials of the Taiwan government. Taiwan is a very important trading partner with the United States, including Florida. On this mission I personally signed agreements on behalf of Florida with Taiwan to sell them phosphate rock and citrus from Florida.

"One morning during the conference I had breakfast at the hotel with Bill Clinton, then governor of Arkansas, along with Governor John Carlin of Kansas. Later in the morning we had an appointment with Premier Chiang Ching-kuo,[7] the leader of Taiwan, in his offices. During our breakfast we discussed the conference, the country of Taiwan, and American issues back home.

"We were graciously welcomed to the premier's office and were formally introduced. During the meeting we talked about world politics, history, and trade between our countries. At one point, he became very interested in our conversation when I told him of my great pleasure at having once met and visited with his mother, Madame Chiang Kai-shek.[8]

"This occurred in Boston in 1958 when I was a top-level staff member with American Farm Bureau. The American Farm Bureau annual convention was being held and it was my job to entertain our two guest speakers while waiting for the scheduled time of their talk. The two speakers were Senator Barry Goldwater and Madame Chiang Kai-shek, the premier's mother. I was privileged to sit for over an hour, listening to the exchange in conversation between these two world leaders. The premier was very interested in my story, as we talked of his mother, that Boston meeting, and that she was educated at Wesleyan College in the U.S."

Wayne relates the story of a major tourist development proposal that arose during his time as lieutenant governor. "While I was lieutenant governor, and performing my job as key promoter of international trade and investment in Florida, I was visited by a young man and his group from England. They presented a plan to build a major tourist attraction near Walt Disney World in Orlando. This is his story.

"It seems that he had worked as a meat cutter in a grocery store while in high school. He had taken advantage of that experience to create a business in home delivery of special cuts of meat. He borrowed 200 English pounds from his father to get started, and from that beginning he grew to ownership of a chain of grocery stores, all successful and growing.

"At the age of thirty-five, the young entrepreneur sold his businesses, clearing $40 million dollars. He soon became restless and took his young wife on their first vacation. They came to Walt Disney World in Florida. His wife explained that as they were driving on I-4 on their way to Disney, he spotted a sign offering a 4400-acre parcel for sale. She said that after he saw that sign, he never wanted to take a vacation—he wanted to answer that ad.

"He found the seller, negotiated a deal, and bought the property before he went home to England. His idea soon became his passion. He wanted to borrow the money to build 'Little England' in Florida on this property. The project was to be a medieval British village, filled with British pubs, unique British shops, international entertainment, and even a half-scale replica of the Big Ben clock looking over the site.

"He later came to me and wanted me to go with him to the financial district in London to lend support, tell of his appetite and passion for the project, and verify the value of the location and his initial investment. I had no ideas on the promise of the attraction, but I did know he owned some of the most valuable 4,000 acres in Florida.

"I agreed to go with him to London and tell of the very valuable property in Florida and confirm that the government would help in every way possible. He sent me a round-trip ticket on the Concord, and another ticket for my travel assistant (Margie). We found it to be a very enjoyable flight. It is difficult to describe traveling at that speed. You can't feel it, and you can't see it, but you get the sensation when you land. After arriving in London, we made our appointments, leaving with good feelings about his reception in the finance centers of London. Everyone was hopeful that we would be hearing Cockney spoken in Florida.

"My real sensation of Concord travel came with our return to Florida. The day began with breakfast in London, a drive to Heathrow, and boarding the Concord. Lunch was served while we were over the Atlantic and had gone supersonic. It was a grand and glorious meal, with many courses of delightful dainties. Our interest was occupied in watching the speed on the indicator located on the bulkhead in front of the cabin.

"Finally, just after the last course, the stewardess announced, 'We will be taking up the dishes for our landing in New York.' The real shocker came a while later when we boarded a flight to Florida, and they were serving breakfast. I found myself totally unable to keep up with a changing world.

"Incidentally, Little England was well on the way, until a downturn in the economy occurred before it was completed. They failed to get into operation, in spite of big expenditures for the village they had built."[9]

During his two terms as lieutenant governor of Florida, Wayne participated in several other events that involved the Concord, the world's first supersonic scheduled passenger air service. Wayne continues, "Sir John King, later named Lord King, was head of British Airways. He had been persuaded by Prime Minister Margaret Thatcher to assume the task of running the airline, with the objective of putting it on a more profitable basis. I had met him on one of my earlier visits to London, for the recognition of the inaugural flight of the Concord to Miami scheduled service.

"During our trade mission with the Tampa Bay group, he had concluded and agreed to establish regular service from London to Tampa. The announcement was scheduled to be made in a few weeks, and I knew how much international attention the Miami announcement had generated. Hoping to create as much attention for the Tampa announcement, while we were in London, I asked for an appointment with him, and it was granted.

"I had done some reviews of his personal interests, and was able to invite him to be the guest of the Tampa Fox Hunting Club on a fox hunt in Florida while he was there for the announcement of the new service and inaugural flight. He thanked the members but declined on the basis of time. The flight was initially not scheduled to be a Concord flight, but I knew that the arrival of a Concord in Tampa would be a huge event. He agreed, and the inaugural flight was converted to be made by the Concord. The event was, of course, a huge occasion. I have never seen more people than that at an airport. There was scarcely standing room on every viewing surface.

"While I was visiting with Sir King, I discussed my interest in World War II, as a participant and as an historian. I told him that one of my heroes from the war was Major General John Frost who, in the Market Garden Campaign, led a small airborne force which captured the east end of the bridge at Arnhem, and held it with very few men, at a terrible cost, for two critical days. Eventually, Frost and all of his men were killed or captured, as the American forces could not get there.

"You might know the story as *A Bridge Too Far*. Sir King told me that General Frost was retired on his farm, just outside of London. To my surprise, just a few days after I got back home, a book came from London in the mail. Its title was *A Jump Too Many* and it was autographed by Major General John Frost. The

Arnhem Bridge operation was the third jump that he had made, and so he titled his book. No question that this is one of my favorite and most prized books. The general died a few months later.

Wayne describes how, under his direction, the Florida Department of Commerce aggressively advertised Florida. "Along with organized trade missions, the Florida Department of Commerce also participated in many international conferences and seminars. These events afforded them the opportunity to advertise and promote the advantages which Florida offered. Funds were budgeted within the Department of Commerce for advertising the virtues of Florida nationally and internationally. A familiar advertisement featuring palm trees, announcing our number one ranking for new business, and with slogans promoting locating businesses in Florida, was featured in media such as the *Wall Street Journal, Forbes*, and *Fortune*. Also, brochures and other printed materials were designed for use at conventions, trade shows, and conferences. We also assisted community-based industrial development specialists across the state in their own local advertising efforts.

"Another ingredient of the concentrated effort to create a coordinated, statewide industrial development system was networking with local industrial recruitment specialists and local chamber of commerce executives. By working with organizations such as the Florida Council of International Development and twelve world trade councils in operation in Florida, and assisting major Florida cities as they organized and conducted their own foreign trade missions, we created an effective, statewide effort.

"As a result of implementing the needed changes, organizing the needed programs and activities, and a lot of coordinated hard work, Florida began to realize tremendous new jobs creation, new industries making significant investments within the state, and a new probusiness attitude. These accomplishments were heralded by Alexander Grant and Company of Chicago, a firm that compiles business climate ratings each year. For four years in a row, 1981, 1982, 1983, and 1984, they ranked Florida as the number one state. Never before had any state won the award two years in a row, much less four. We were recognized as having the sixth-fastest-growing labor force, with a low percentage of unionization, and as a leader in creation of international trade zones.

"I reminded the media that, during our campaign for our first term, we had pledged to create 50,000 new jobs and had already created 103,000 after the first three years. I told them that I felt that Florida's new probusiness climate would create the 175,000 new jobs I was promising. I also reviewed efforts which were underway to woo a part of the movie industry to Florida.

"In an article which appeared in the *Journal of Commerce* in September of 1981, Bob and I were given credit for the 'remarkable transition' which was occurring in the Florida economy. It described how the state had changed from being 'antibusiness' to being a leading 'probusiness' state in only two and one half years. It stated that international trade had risen to over $30 billion, and exports had risen to $18 billion.

"Our many foreign trade missions were credited for this growth. At the same time, industrial recruitment had brought in 282 new plants for a capital investment of $2.14 billion and creating 57,770 new jobs. Simultaneously, expansions of existing businesses had created another 27,062 jobs. It also explained that the growth had not been localized in one area of the state, but had instead involved all parts of Florida.

"In 1972 the total volume of international trade in Florida was about $2 billion dollars. In 1984 it had increased to over $20 billion dollars. At that point, almost a quarter of Miami's total economy was being generated by international activities entering through the Miami International Airport and local ports. Additionally, international banking had risen as a new industry for Florida.

"By the end of 1985, new international investments had created tens of thousands of jobs in Florida, and the foreign investments had added millions to state tax revenues. I am proud of what we accomplished and gladdened by the positive impact our work had in improving living circumstances for thousands of Florida's workers."

Because of the national media recognition about the remarkable accomplishments in jobs creation in Florida by the Graham-Mixson administration, and the role that Wayne Mixson had played in leading the effort, Wayne began to be in demand as a qualified speaker on the subject of industrial recruitment. He was invited to speak before the historic Chicago Rotary Club. Wayne describes the event, "My subject was an overview of the progress Florida was making in becoming a leading state for industrial development and international trade. I began by explaining that a worldwide transition into a global economy is beginning, and that Florida has been at the forefront of this new movement for the past decade. I explained that, as termed a 'mega-trend' by author John Naisbitt, the state of Florida, and eventually the nation, are becoming immersed in an economic transformation.

"I told the history of these changes by relating what Florida had experienced during the 1973-74 oil embargo and ensuing recession, in which Florida had fallen into a deeper decline than the rest of the nation. And the fall lasted longer for us than the rest of the country. Our state unemployment rate was consistently higher than the national average, and our state economy stayed depressed through most of the 1970s. Then, when another recession hit the nation during the early 1980s, we noticed a new phenomenon. While the rest of the country experienced a serious economic fall, we only had a slowdown. Through it all, our economy performed better than the rest of the nation. Something had changed. I explained that new technology had become the leading manufacturing sector in Florida, having replaced our traditional leader, food processing. We had risen to the ranking of seventh largest high technology manufacturer in the nation. We employed more high-tech workers than the next three southern states of Georgia, North Carolina, and Vrrginia combined.

"I explained that, without our knowledge, the new global economy had been entering the business sector of Florida's economy.

It was counteracting the impact of the prevalent recession in heavy industry. I identified three major forces of the new global economy that were making a strong positive impact in Florida. The first was the rapid internationalizing of our economy. In the preceding decade international trade volume had grown from $2 billion to over $18 billion. The second force was the beginning of lifestyle and perceptual changes. The third force was the great strides gained in technologies. Even with persistent hard times during the preceding ten years, Florida had an average growth of 5 to 6 percent. New jobs in Florida had grown at almost three times the national rate. Our manufacturing jobs had increased 40 percent while they were decreasing nationally.

"I related how the internationalization of our state began in the 1950s with the Cuban migration, as Castro took over that island nation. Today that bilingual Cuban presence has turned Miami into a true international center, and a focal point of connection between the United States and the entire Caribbean Basin. It has become the financial center of Latin America. Also, many large multinational corporations have established regional headquarters in South Florida. Over ten percent of our state population speaks Spanish. Miami is recognized as one of three emerging 'global cities,' along with Paris and Honolulu.

"I compared Miami as an international transportation hub just as Chicago was for linking the east coast with the west coast. I told the Rotarians that Miami was also becoming an international communications hub between the U.S. and the southern hemisphere. With Miami serving as the major point of contact, our inflow of international businesses began to spread throughout the state. Simultaneously the state enjoyed a tremendous expansion in international tourism.

"I told how Florida has evolved into the leading high technology manufacturer for the Southeast. We were then seventh in the nation for high-tech jobs, and our growth was outpacing every other major state. I described how Florida now had two high-technology centers which stretched for over a hundred miles.

Our 'silicon coast' stretches from Miami to Palm Beach, and had dozens of very large plants and many more smaller supporting manufacturers. Then the 'electronics belt' stretches from the Space Coast through Orlando, and over to Tampa. I stated that these companies had located in Florida because of many lower costs, but also because Florida offered an attractive lifestyle for the engineering and technical type of talents these businesses needed. Florida is attractive because it is a great place to work and a great place to play.

"I also mentioned our new, growing robotics technology facilities. We had attracted three major robotics research companies, General Electronic, IBM, and Westinghouse, and had opened a robotics research center at the University of Florida. Of course, I lauded the fact that Florida has the first spaceport in the world at Cape Canaveral, and a new High Technology Demonstration Facility at Walt Disney World's Epcot Center.

"I explained that another unique and important aspect of Florida's astounding growth had been our emphasis on creating a system of managed growth that enabled industry, agriculture, and the environment to all thrive simultaneously. A beautiful, healthy environment is essential for the continuing growth of our state tourism industry.

"I emphasized the importance of agriculture in Florida and how we had designed measures to preserve and protect farming in the state. We had established the Greenbelt Law which created a fair basis of taxation for development and farming, and had led the way in environmental protections which were fair to the farmer. I also brought up the fact that Florida leads the nation in open government laws, which we call 'Sunshine Laws,' which make most government activities accessible for citizens to review.

"I couldn't keep from bragging a little as I told the group that Florida had won the Alexander Grant and Company annual designation as the state with the "Best Business Climate for Manufacturers' for four years in a row because of our low level of taxation, reasonable regulatory climate, and general probusiness attitude.

"Finally, I discussed our emerging film and television industries, and the future potentials in satellite television transmission to the Caribbean and Latin America. I closed with pledging that Florida stood ready to transport and export the products which were produced in their area. We wanted a relationship of fellowship and cooperation with them. I told them that whether they came to work with us or to play with us, they were always welcome in Florida."

These dramatic accomplishments for Florida's economy would help provide much-needed jobs for future generations of Florida citizens. Wayne took great pride and personal satisfaction from knowing that his work had significantly improved the lives of the families of many. These new industries and jobs were helping those workers he had seen displaced by agricultural technology. Today, Florida's dynamic ports and prominence in international commerce are all part of the Graham-Mixson legacy.

Working with the Legislative Branch

Maintaining a close, positive working relationship with the legislative branch of government is an important aspect of any successful governor's administration. Since Bob and Wayne were both former legislators, and were quite familiar with how the legislative branch functioned, they were keenly aware of how important this relationship was to their success. When the administration began to encounter some problems in getting desired legislation passed, Governor Graham once again turned to Wayne. He delegated the task of being the official liaison with the legislature to his lieutenant governor. Wayne responded quickly by accomplishing a reorganization of the lobbying staff, and stressing a culture aimed at creating a more personal approach in developing legislative support for their initiatives. This change did much to aid implementation of their agenda. Wayne describes this important role.

"Early in 1980 Governor Graham added another duty to my job description. He made me the head lobbyist for the Graham administration, as it worked with the Florida House and Senate on needed legislation. During the preceding year Bob had encountered increasing difficulties in getting legislation which he was promoting moved through committees, and onto the floor for passage. Knowing that I had a complete knowledge of the inner workings of both chambers, was recognized as a moderating force, and had retained close ties with many legislators, he decided to ask me to assume this additional role.

"In the 1979 regular session, and during the following special tax session, Governor Graham's legislative agenda had encountered serious problems. That history resulted in this reorganization and this new role for me. As a lobbyist for our legislative programs, I knew the importance of assessing the number of legislators who were willing to sponsor the propositions early in the process, and then working hard to accumulate enough commitments to assure passage, before a vote was ever taken. Previously, Bob had endured some surprise outcomes because his lobbyists were not taking this approach. Also, the process of promoting new legislation would be changed to a more personal contact process, instead of a formal, educational system. I also made several staff changes in order to remove some of the lobbyists who were not being well received by legislators, and then adding those who had the personal attributes and backgrounds to be successful in working with everyone."

Helping Haiti

Wayne describes another role he fulfilled as lieutenant governor. "In 1981 I was given the task of spearheading an agricultural mission to the impoverished country of Haiti. Florida was experiencing an ongoing problem of stopping boatloads of desperate Haitian refugees from landing on the shores of Florida. After visiting Haiti and seeing the terrible conditions which existed for the population there, Bob decided to sponsor a program which would assist the people in improving their living conditions, and thus reduce the incentive to flee to Florida.

"At the time I had never been to Haiti, but was very aware of the history and condition of the nation. My project began with a meeting in Miami with Haitian embassy officials, State Department aides, and local business interests. The meeting focused on short-term economic relief, although other, long-range, programs were discussed. We also discussed adding Haiti to cruise ship itineraries and the potential markets for Haitian handicrafts and arts.

"It was at this meeting I learned that 80 percent of Haiti's population lives on small farms, yet the country has no fertilizer mix plant. I also was informed of the tremendous amount of soil erosion the country experienced as a result of deforestation, and the ongoing impact of this condition on the rivers of the country. I was very aware of the enormity of the needs, and stressed the fact that we were not going to be able to 'accomplish miracles,' but hoped to help.

"Next I traveled to Haiti and met with president-for-life, Jean-Claude Duvalier, to discuss technical aid programs for the impoverished nation. During the meeting we discussed the continuing U.S. policy of interdicting boatloads of Haitian refugees who were attempting to reach Florida's shores. We also discussed the treatment of those refugees once they were returned to Haiti. He pledged that they would only punish those who were trafficking in refugees.

"Included in my group to Haiti were over two dozen technical experts and businessmen who conducted a round of meetings with local officials and representatives from the Haitian business community. They explored ways of creating programs to improve Haiti's economy.

"I served as chairman of the FAVA/CA[10] Executive Advisory Committee and helped accomplish a grant agreement with the U.S. Agency for International Development (USAID). From this activity we obtained a $156,000 grant to help poor people in the Caribbean nations. A part of this grant was used to establish a resource center for delivery of technical assistance to Haiti and Caribbean countries.

"In 1982 trade between Florida and the nations of the Caribbean basin was more than $3.9 billion dollars, about 24 percent of Florida's total international trade. The Caribbean nations were thus an important component of our international trade programs.

"Each year we conducted a Governor's Conference on World Trade and gave awards to the companies and individuals who were leading the way in expanding Florida's growing international involvement. This was just another component of our effort in the international arena.

"A normal, Christian person with any sympathy for the suffering of his fellow man cannot visit Haiti and avoid being impacted by the plight of the majority of the population of that impoverished nation. Their condition is largely the result of over two hundred years of inept, corrupt governments. They have endured successive regimes of selfish, corrupt, and uncaring dictators supported by a cadre of similarly minded politicians. Their plight cannot be permanently corrected until the nation is governed by an ethical, honest, and benevolent government. The real solution in Haiti is jobs, as it is in all failed economies. But no significant industrial investments will be made until the political problems are resolved. Haiti desperately needs the emergence of a George Washington."

In this discussion, Wayne once again reveals his deep, personal concern for the plight of the unfortunates in any society. The frustration he felt as a result of his inability to really accomplish the needed solutions is reflected in his comments concerning Haiti's history of political corruption.

Liaison with Local Governments

Both Bob and Wayne were aware of the many difficulties that existed in the relationship between the state government and local county and municipal governments. Wayne was assigned the job of functioning as the primary liaison between their administration and these local governments. "One of the needs which Bob and I had identified during our campaign travels was the difficulties that many local county commissions and municipalities were having in working with the complexities of the state government and its bureaucracies. We pledged to implement measures which would make it much easier for local officials to work with the state organizations in order to solve problems and meet needs. This was one of the initial tasks directed to me for implementation as we took office.

"One means of accomplishing this objective was to enhance communication between the administration and these local entities. A key element of this effort was starting with a series of day-long regional forums which included local officials and owners of small businesses. In 1984 we conducted four of these forums and expanded that to eleven in 1985.

"We listed and ranked the issues which were brought forward during these work sessions. These were then given to the governor and each legislator for consideration. At that time some of the major concerns of small businesses across the state were: skyrocketing costs for liability insurance, decreased availability of carriers, unemployment compensation taxes, workman's compensation premiums, review of sales tax exemptions, excessive government paperwork, rules and regulations, simplification of tax forms and wage reports, the need for industrial job training in schools, and increasing programs to assist small businesses with technical and financial needs.

"Inside the Florida Department of Commerce, we enhanced a portion of the Division of Economic Development in order to provide better services. Also, the Bureau of Business Assistance, with its Offices of Finance, Entrepreneurship, and Business Services, was used to assist small businesses in their struggles."

The Unitary Tax

The team of Bob Graham and Wayne Mixson realized great success in implementation of their defined agenda programs because they worked out a method to divide their areas of responsibility. With the many complex issues, varied interests, lack of communication caused by separate schedules and responsibilities, and complications created by travel, it is difficult for all administrations to avoid problems. Such a situation arose over a special tax called the unitary tax, which was created to provide needed funding for education. However, since it placed a state levy on overseas profits realized by doing commerce with Florida, it would negatively impact the work underway in the Department of Commerce promoting increased international trade. This created a situation that could have damaged the relationship between Wayne and Bob. Wayne discusses the event.

"Although Governor Bob Graham and I came from two different worlds, were supported by vastly different constituencies, and held very diverse opinions on many issues, our mutual respect and appreciation for each other enabled us to always resolve and work through issues as they arose. Prior to forming the Graham-Mixson ticket in our first campaign, we discussed these differences and how we could work together to not allow these issues to create problems for us as we implemented programs. During the eight years we shared the top positions in the state, the issue involving the unitary tax tested our abilities more than any other issue.

"The unitary tax, which was enacted in a one-day special session during the summer of 1983, placed a levy on the overseas profits earned by businesses doing business in Florida. I was against the tax because it had a significant negative effect on our ability to attract new foreign industries to Florida. This tax also potentially had a negative impact on the agricultural community which was so important in our state. It worked in contradiction to the objectives of the Department of Commerce, which I was directing.

"Bob Graham had sponsored the passage of the tax because it offered a potential of creating $95 million in new state revenue, which he wanted to use as part of a $200 million funding package for needed educational programs. The regular session had ended without passage of an education budget. I initiated a call for repeal of the tax. The hurriedly passed bill made Florida one of only twelve states with such an antibusiness tax, and the only southern state with the tax.

"I publicly stressed my opposition to the tax. This was not a demonstration of disloyalty to Bob Graham. My position on the issue of the tax was instead motivated by my unwillingness to support anything that worked against the objectives which I had been seeking for my entire political career. It was based on the fact that I had to be my own man and had to stand for my personal beliefs. Bob understood that fact. Because of the growing uproar over the tax, he agreed to form a special nineteen-member commission to study the impact of the tax. Companies such as Citicorp, IBM, Westinghouse, and others made public statements that the presence of the tax would cause them to reevaluate their investments in Florida.

"The push to repeal the tax gained momentum throughout 1983 and 1984 as many organizations, businesses, Associated Industries of Florida, and even many of Graham's cabinet members, spoke out publicly favoring a bill to repeal. Facing this growing opposition, Bob finally softened his position on the issue, stating that he would go along with repeal if a suitable substitute funding source for his education programs could be found.

"In December of 1984, the legislature passed a bill repealing the unitary tax and changing the state corporate tax from 5.0 percent to 5.5 percent to offset the lost revenue. The bill was moved to the governor's desk for signing. Bob agreed to sign the bill and repeal the controversial tax. A few weeks earlier, a vice president of the

Sony Corporation promised a flow of 'golden eggs' into Florida from Japan as a result of the repeal. He stated that because of the growing trade deficit, three major Japanese companies were going to make investments in the U.S. of $240 million and 2,000 jobs in the coming year in states which had no unitary tax. He made these remarks in a private meeting with Bob Graham. I think that the governor decided to go along with the repeal at that time.

"When I made my public announcement regarding my support of the repeal effort, Bob was on a trip to Asia, including a trip to Japan where he met with business leaders. Initially Bob expressed displeasure at my announcement, and our disagreement became very public. But our mutual respect for each other, and our ongoing friendship, enabled us to heal the wounds as the issue was resolved. Bob put it clearly when he said, 'It is like a marriage where occasionally the husband and wife have a disagreement. In our case, it is a public one.'"

No Casinos

The casino gambling issue has always been a controversial, recurring proposal for the Florida legislature. As tourism grew in South Florida, and the number of hotels and other tourism-dependent businesses increased, the lobbying efforts to achieve legislation of casino gambling intensified. With the revenues realized from legalized gambling in Las Vegas as an example, the support for the measure was strengthened.

Throughout his political career, Wayne had always made his position on this issue very clear. "During our initial campaign for the governor's office, in numerous campaign speeches Bob and I proclaimed one of our policies to be 'no casinos.' This troublesome issue rose to the surface twice during our eight years of office, and in the manner of a difficult-to-kill garden snake, has risen on occasions during the succeeding thirty years. Bob and I successfully thwarted the movement while we were in office.

"The most vigorous campaign favoring permitting casino operations to open in Florida came in 1986, when the proponents submitted Amendment 2, which would have legalized the activities. A group named Citizens for County Choice on Casinos was formed to promote the amendment. As a major component of their pro-casino effort, they invested approximately $300,000 on creating a series of commercials for broadcast at major cities throughout the state. The commercials related how much tax revenue was escaping in casino operations on cruise ships that were operating out of Florida's ports. It criticized newspapers and other media which editorialized against casinos, but at the same time enjoyed selling cruise ship advertising which featured casinos on board. Also, the fact that many state escrow funds are invested in companies which operate casinos was noted. The commercials emphasized the hypocrisy of much of the opposition.

"On the other side of the issue was the 'No Casinos Grassroots Army' which I participated in as vice chairman, while Jack Eckerd was appointed as chairman by Governor Graham. I had held the same position in the organization in 1982, when the pro-casino group had attempted but failed to get the issue on the ballot. Many Florida organizations, individuals, and businesses such as Walt Disney World, the *Tampa Tribune*, Jack Eckerd Corporation, and various state banks supported the anti casino effort. The group was organized on a regional basis with chapters in several of Florida's major cities. I made supportive presentations at all of them during the effort to have the amendment defeated.

"Personally, I was adamantly against the move to allow casinos because of the fact that gambling seems to always lure a significant percentage of the uneducated, poor segment of the population. Casinos plunder those who can least afford to lose. Additionally, I believe that casinos foster crime and corruption. Florida thrives on family tourism, and casinos do not fit into that environment. I felt that casinos would be bad for future industrial development in Florida.

"Jack Eckerd chartered a Boeing 747 to take a large contingent, which included gubernatorial candidates, legislators, media, and others, to Atlantic City, New Jersey, in order to see a decaying and corrupt city, which had resulted from the presence of casinos. We felt that if the condition and history of Atlantic City were advertised, few of Florida's voters would approve the proposed amendment in the upcoming November election. The amendment would allow counties to decide by referendum whether or not they wanted to allow casino gambling in hotels with over 500 rooms. In 1978, while I was in the legislature, Florida's voters defeated a casino amendment which would have allowed casinos along a sixteen-mile strip running from Hollywood to Miami Beach. This time the amendment would allow casinos throughout the state. Of course, Miami had many hotels that would qualify for housing a casino, but nearly half of the qualifying hotels were on I-4 between Orlando and St. Petersburg, in the center of our state.

"The anti-casino advertising project featured professionally prepared commercials. One which ran in South Florida featured Janet Reno narrating the arguments against the amendment, the second featured Jack Eckerd and was run in Central Florida, and the third featured me and was run in North Florida. The script for each was the same. After displaying the dilemma in New Jersey, they included the plea, 'Please don't let this happen here. Don't gamble with Florida.'

"During this campaign against casinos I also worked actively with a contingent of top law enforcement officials in the state. With these officials, we conducted a series of media events where we explained how the introduction of casino gambling into Florida would open the door for increased organized crime activities, would increase crime rates, and would offer new opportunities for money laundering through casino operations.

"When the November vote came, the amendment was soundly defeated. I take solace in knowing that I played an important role in helping keep casino gambling out of our state. I know we are better off today because of our actions in 1986."

Protecting Florida's Environment

During the two terms of the Graham-Mixson administration, Wayne focused primarily on leading initiatives for industrial development, jobs creation, fair taxation, and improving local-state coordination. Meanwhile, Bob led the forward movement in areas where he held deep personal interests, such as urban issues, environmental protection, and education. Through it all, they coordinated and assisted each other to achieve these objectives.

Under their leadership, Florida developed and implemented a series of new environmental protection initiatives and moved their state into a place of recognition as one of the leading states in the nation for environmental protection programs.

Among the most notable of these programs was a network of appointed regional state commissions, with taxing and permitting authority, to manage and assure water quality throughout the state. They were given authority to conduct impact studies on all commercial development before issuing water management permits allowing them to proceed with construction.

Wayne was cautiously supportive of the measure. He studied the proposal carefully, evaluating how much negative impact this new permitting requirement would have on his jobs creation efforts, the agricultural sector, and the public at large. Wayne had always felt a great concern for Florida's fragile environment, and realized the need for strict oversight of Florida's fresh water systems.

After suggesting a few modifications, Wayne publicly supported the bill that created the Water Management System. "One stipulation that I requested was the removal of a proposed Water Management Commission for Northwest Florida, including the Panhandle. I did not feel that we had enough development or population density in that part of the state to justify the cost. However, when the finalized bill came to the floor of the legislature, the Northwest Florida Water Management District had been included. At that point the momentum was so great that I could not stop it."

Another lasting environmental measure that was enacted during the Graham-Mixson administration was the Save the Florida Manatee movement. As the state population had grown, so had the volume of fishing and water sport activities on Florida's waters. Much of the state's inland water is the habitat of the unique, docile, water mammal, the manatee. Frequent injuries from boat propellers were killing these peaceful creatures by the thousands, endangering the survival of the species.

Governor Bob Graham led a movement that resulted in passage of regulations designed to control boating in the manatee's habitat, to restrict activities in fresh water springs where the creatures thrived, and other steps to protect this animal and its habitat. As a result of this action, today the Florida Manatee is thriving. These environmental programs are another part of the Graham-Mixson legacy.

Mixson for Governor

As the Graham-Mixson administration entered the last year of its second term, both men began to consider their future. Bob Graham, who was fifteen years younger than Wayne, was not ready to retire. He began to plan for a campaign to capture a seat representing Florida in the U.S. Senate. For Wayne, the choice was more difficult. He was entering the latter phase of his life and was financially able to enjoy a wonderful retirement with Margie. At the same time, he was ideally positioned to win the upcoming election and the governorship. Wayne describes his feelings.

"As 1986 arrived and the end of our final term approached, there was growing anticipation that I would run for governor as Bob Graham stepped down. In fact, in one attempt to draft me as a candidate, a group of supporters met and began a fund drive for my campaign. They took this action without my approval, and I subsequently asked them to return the money they had collected.

"By this time, I was well recognized throughout the state, and our administration was being recognized for creating a good period of management and growth in Florida. We had made great progress in jobs creation, educational improvements, taxation, business regulation, and environment protection. I felt that I had a good chance of winning the governor's position if I chose to run. The only well-known potential opposition candidate was Bob Martinez[11] of Tampa.

"One important factor in my decision not to run for governor was what had already been accomplished during my work as the lieutenant governor during the Graham administration. My strongest motivation had always been to convert Florida from having an antibusiness attitude into one of the leading states in industrial development and jobs creation. I wanted to bring those jobs to Florida in order to provide a better life for those thousands of farm families who were displaced as technology modernized the farming industries. If this task had remained undone, I would have run for governor. However, I felt we had already accomplished that goal.

"At this juncture I had twenty years of public service behind me, and I was in my early sixties. Margie and I discussed our options as we struggled with the decision about declaring our intent to run for the governor's position and launch into organizing a campaign. Our other option was to begin to ease into retirement, travel, enjoy our relationship, and 'smell the roses'. After much discussion and consideration, we decided on the latter choice. I would not seek the governorship.

"Meanwhile, Bob Graham had decided to run for the U.S. Senate. I was soon to find that if he won election in November, it would create an unusual situation for me."

Endnotes

1. Park Wright III (born 1921, died 2001) was the former executive vice president of Lykes Bros., Inc., the vast holding company with interests in citrus, sugar, banking, ranching, meat packing, natural gas distribution, and construction. With major landholdings in Florida and Texas, they are among the largest private landholders in the nation. Mr. Park was an army pilot in World War II. In 1944 he was shot down over Stuttgart, Germany, and spent nine months as a prisoner of war, until the war ended.

2. Schloss Vollrads is a castle and wine estate in the Rheingau wine-growing region in Germany. They have been making wine for over 800 years.

3. Maxwell Milton Rabb (born 1910, died 2002) was born in Boston, Massachusetts, and earned an AB and LLB from Harvard. In 1944 Rabb joined the U.S. Naval Reserve and served as a lieutenant until 1946. Rabb became part of the Eisenhower White House staff during the early 1950s. He served as the U.S. ambassador to Italy from 1981 until 1989.

4. The Great Hall of the People is located at the western edge of the Tiananmen Square, Beijing. It is used for legislative and ceremonial activities by the People's Republic of China and the Communist Party of China. Along with many major national political and social events, the Great Hall has been used for meetings with foreign dignitaries on state or working visits. The hall will seat 10,000 people in its auditorium, which is adorned with a galaxy of lights on its ceiling and a dramatic red star in its middle.

5. The Jin Jiang Hotel in Shanghai is one of the most prestigious five-star hotels in downtown Shanghai. The hotel has received over 500 state visitors and foreign government heads. It covers an area of over 30,000 square miles and overlooks 16,500 square miles of greenbelt, including beautiful gardens.

6. Taipei, literally meaning "North of Tai(wan)," officially known as Taipei City, is the capital city and a special municipality of Taiwan. Sitting at the northern tip of Taiwan, Taipei City is an enclave of the municipality of New Taipei City. It is about 25 km southwest of the northern port city of Keelung. Most of the city is located on the Taipei Basin, an ancient lakebed.

7. Chiang Ching-kuo (born April 1910, died January 1988). Politician and leader. Was the son of Chiang Kai-shek and held numerous posts in the government of the Republic of China, from 1949 ji-om the island of Taiwan. He succeeded his father to power, serving as premier of the Republic of China from 1972 until 1978, and president of the Republic of China from 1978 until his death in 1988. Under his tenure, the government of the Republic of China, although still authoritarian, became more open and tolerant of political dissent. Toward the end of his life, Chiang relaxed many government controls on the press and free speech, and put native Taiwanese in positions of power, including his successor, Lee Teng-hui, who furthered the course of democratic reforms.

8. Madame Chiang Kai-shek (born March 1898, died October 2003) was a first lady of the Republic of China, the wife of Generalissimo and President Chiang Kai-shek. She played a prominent role in the politics of the Republic of China, and was the sister-in-law of Sun Yat-sen, the founder and leader of the Republic of China. She was active in the civic life of her country, and held many honorary and active positions, including chairman of Fu Jen Catholic University.

9. Little England Theme Park. Located down the street from Walt Disney World in Orlando, Florida, this proposed 100-acre theme park would offer a taste of the history and culture of England. With a medieval castle as its centerpiece, development of this multi-attraction park began with the construction of a preview village. The preview buildings were built from a group of 300-year-old barn structures which were disassembled in England and reconstructed here. Many of the original architectural elements, including heavy lumber framing, clay roof tiles, wooden wall shingles, and chimney pots, were reused. Nearing completion of the preview village construction, financial circumstances left the development unable to open.

10. The Florida Association for Volunteer Action in the Caribbean and the Americas, Inc. (FAVA/CA), is a private, not-for-profit organization formed in 1982 by Florida governor Bob Graham. Florida International Volunteer Corps is the only program of its kind in the country. A state appropriation provides a funding base for an estimated 100 volunteer missions to Latin America and the Caribbean each year.

11. Robert "Bob" Martinez was the 40th governor of Florida from 1987 to 1991; he was the first person of Spanish ancestry to be elected to the state's top office. Prior to that, he was the mayor of Tampa from 1979 to 1986.

CHAPTER TEN

JOHN WAYNE MIXSON—FLORIDA'S 39TH GOVERNOR

1989

A Historic Situation

It would seem that Wayne Mixson was predestined to become the governor of Florida, even though he had publicly announced his intent to spend his retirement years with Margie instead of capitalizing on his position as lieutenant governor and seeking a probable election to the governorship. Fate was to assure that honor was still going to be bestowed upon him.

Wayne explains, "During our last year in office, Bob Graham launched a campaign to become Florida's U.S. senator. In November of 1988 he won that seat in the federal government, and Bob Martinez simultaneously became the governor-elect of Florida. This victory created a situation in Florida's government that had never been encountered in the history of the state. Because Governor Graham's term as the new senator representing Florida in the U.S. Senate began in Washington on January 3, three days before his term officially ended as governor of Florida on January 6, he was forced to resign his governorship three days before his term ended. This was a requirement of the Resign to Run Law. The succession provision in the Florida Constitution required that I, as the lieutenant governor, be immediately elevated to the position of governor if the elected governor resigned for any reason. Thus, by law I was to be officially thrust into the top position in the state—for three days.

"In order to follow protocol and thus preserve the established traditions for the office of governor of Florida, it was decided that all of the normal ceremonial agenda for the transition would be followed. That meant that we were to hold an inauguration parade and an inaugural ball on the day Bob resigned and I took the oath of office.

"Ironically, while I was ceremoniously assuming the office of governor, the governor-elect, Bob Martinez, was busily preparing to move into the governor's mansion when he took office on January 7. Simultaneously, upon his resignation the Graham family was in the process of moving to Washington, D.C. Although the situation was unique, I was very proud and honored to have the distinction of serving as the 39th governor of the wonderful state of Florida, even if it was for only three days."

On January 3, 1989, with Margie standing proudly at his side holding the family Bible, Wayne was formally administered the oath of office in an official ceremony. In his inaugural address, Wayne reviewed many of the accomplishments of the Graham-Mixson administration's eight years of leadership of the executive branch of Florida's government. Some of the achievements he proudly listed included:

- Brought over 800 new industries to Florida, creating over 1.4 million much-needed new jobs
- Caused Florida to be recognized worldwide for its international banking and trade
- Made Florida the third-largest producer of television and movie material
- Enhanced Florida's position as the world's number one tourist destination

- Made Florida have among the lowest rate of taxation in the United States
- Created a pro-industry environment by lowering regulation and taxation
- Used proceeds of a strong state economy to enhance education, which supported needs of new industries
- Doubled the number of engineering graduates in the university system
- Used the proceeds of a strong state economy to afford implementation of innovative programs to enhance and protect Florida's environment. These included such programs as Save Our Rivers, Save Our Coasts, Save the Manatees, and Save our Everglades, passage of the Wetlands Protection Act, and creation of five water management districts
- Used proceeds of a strong state economy to enhance state-funded social assistance programs
- Established programs to create a healthy blend for coexistence of agricultural progress and urban growth

Wayne also expressed how humbled and proud he was to have had the opportunity to serve the citizens of Florida during his twenty-year career. When Wayne finished his speech he was given a long standing ovation as a tribute for his accomplishments. It was an emotional moment for most in attendance. They realized that the legacy of his work as a legislator, lieutenant governor, and governor would serve the people of Florida for many generations. He was widely appreciated as a great Floridian.

Wayne did enjoy the unforgettable experience of becoming the governor of Florida, taking control of the state's highest office, and sitting at the governor's desk, if only for a moment. It was a fitting tribute and ending to his productive career of service to the citizens of Florida.

Throughout those twenty years of public service to the state of Florida, Wayne had always worked diligently to enhance the quality of life for the citizens of the state through jobs creation from industrial development, to protect and expand the agricultural industry of the state, to provide excellent management of Florida's astounding population growth, and to simultaneously protect the unique environment of Florida. His accomplishments in these areas will long endure.

Soon it was over, and the incoming governor, Bob Martinez, was ceremoniously sworn into the governor's office. As friends and peers said a sad farewell, Wayne and Margie left the state capital, and began a well-deserved life of retirement.

CHAPTER ELEVEN

RETIREMENT YEARS

1987–Present

On January 7, 1987, Bob Martinez became governor of Florida and Wayne and Margie officially left politics and entered their planned retirement. Once again, they were embarking on another phase of their lives. Unknown at the time, they had over thirty years of shared retirement experiences ahead of them.

Throughout his life Wayne had never smoked, had only politely sipped a few social drinks, ate good foods, and stayed in reasonably good shape. As a result of this healthy lifestyle, and good genetics, Wayne has been able to enjoy a long and rewarding retirement period with Margie, family, and friends. Wayne celebrated his 95th and 96th birthdays while this biography was being written.

As is the case with most people when they retire from a busy career, Wayne soon found that what he had actually done was merely change the venue of his work. Retirement evokes visions of sitting on a swing in the backyard, watching the squirrels play and waiting for a hummingbird to land on the feeder. Most of the time that is not the case, as private work and life's demands continue to consume your time.

Wayne describes becoming a retiree, "In my case, I once again returned to the farm. Additionally, I continued to hold positions on several corporate boards and in numerous organizations. In combination, I still had little idle time. For Margie, there was little change of lifestyle. She remained active in many charitable organizations, and always enjoyed an active social schedule with friends.

"All of my life I have been a farmer at heart. My career as a legislator and then as lieutenant governor had been rewarding and interesting, but my roots remained imbedded in agriculture. The family farm in Jackson County had always remained as a financial support and backup career while I served in Florida politics. When I retired from public service in 1987, it was only natural that once again I would return to the farm.

"I was fortunate to have developed a very capable staff at the farm which was able to properly operate and manage whether I was involved or not. When I left politics I was sixty-five, an age where the manual labor of farming was becoming a hardship. I realized that it was time for us to sell the farm, since Margie and I had no children to continue the farm in the Mixson name."

Wayne and Margie had traveled extensively during earlier phases of their lives. While Wayne was a top executive with the Farm Bureau organization, the work had required continual national and international travel. Then while he was lieutenant governor, he focused on jobs creation, trade enhancement, and industrial recruitment. During those years he frequently represented Florida at official international events. In addition, he led many trade missions to foreign countries during that era.

Wayne continues, "Margie and I had always enjoyed traveling. While I was in the legislature and serving as lieutenant governor, we had the opportunity to travel together on several occasions. We decided that we would share experiencing interesting parts of the world together after we retired and were still healthy and energetic. We wanted to create lasting memories from these shared excursions.

"During the summer of 1981 Margie and I went on a two-week vacation trip to Greece. We toured the entire country and visited many ancient ruins and beautiful sites. A few months later we traveled to Philadelphia and attended the five-day national Lieutenant Governor's Conference. For many years in retirement, we continued to travel the world, often renewing old friendships, and always enjoying the sights and cultures of other countries."

Wayne's lifetime has involved several varied careers. His resume would recognize him as a leading Florida agriculturist, as a top executive for the Farm Bureau, as a leading legislator in Florida's politics, as a longtime member and chairman of the Florida House of Representatives Agricultural Committee, as lieutenant governor for eight years, and as governor for three days. Each of these roles resulted in much recognition for his service and work, and the accumulation of a wide assortment of plaques, trophies, and official documents. Wayne sincerely felt appreciation for each of these, but it was a physical impossibility for him to properly display them all. Out of necessity, Wayne carefully filled a storage building behind his house with these valued mementos.

Wayne speaks humbly about these awards, "As a byproduct of twenty years of public service, it is natural to receive many awards for service. I have a storage building filled with a multitude of cherished plaques, medals, certificates, and documents bestowing gratitude and recognition upon me for my service. Many of these are traditional awards which are always given at the end of a period of service by an individual. These would be awards recognizing service as chairman of a committee, president of an organization, or even membership in a group. These are meaningful and appreciated, but the awards which mean the most are those 'special' awards which are created just to honor you for some special achievement or for lifetime service.

"The awards I received during my years of public service were too numerous to include all of them in this listing. Some of the more notable recognitions I was privileged to receive during my lifetime included: Dedication of Highway 73 in Jackson County as 'Wayne Mixson Highway' by the Florida legislature; the acknowledgment of 'Wayne Mixson Day' (a State of Alabama legislative bill); and the creation of another Wayne Mixson Day in Bonifay, Florida, October 8, 1981).

"Agricultural awards always had a special significance to me. Some of these awards included the following: Jaycee Good Government Award, 1967; Legislative Service Award from Florida Farm Bureau Federation, 1972; Gamma Sigma Delta Honor Society of Agriculture at University of Florida; Award of Merit for Distinguished Service to Agriculture, 1974; Florida Farm Bureau Distinguished Service Award, 1974; Florida Association of Community College Legislative Service Award, 1974; and the Florida Thoroughbred Horse Breeders Association Award for Service to the Industry and to Agriculture, 1974."

During the "Golden Years of the Florida Legislature," which included the years in which the new constitution was penned, the reorganization through constitutional amendments in the ensuing session, and many key legislative acts that have enabled Florida to enjoy prosperity and rapid growth in a managed, well-designed manner, one of the key legislators through this critical era was Representative John Wayne Mixson. His dedicated work as repeated chairman of the Agricultural Committee led to enactment of a body of legislation that has protected and nurtured Florida's agricultural industries for almost fifty years.

His legislative works included the design and sponsorship of taxation legislation that enabled Florida's unprecedented development to occur without overtaxing and ruining adjacent farm operations. This was accomplished by allowing land to be taxed based on usage instead of location. He also was instrumental in passage of the Greenbelt Law that allowed land to have a low, agricultural property tax classification as long as it is used for farming, even if the owner does not actually live on the properties.

While he was the lieutenant governor and the acting director of the Florida Department of Commerce, Wayne's activities made Florida a leading state in foreign trade. His trade missions opened lucrative new markets for Florida's agricultural products. As a result, agriculture expanded and prospered, making it an even more important element of Florida's expanding economy. Also, he sponsored and helped enact funding for Florida's outstanding agricultural schools, including creating the School of Veterinary Medicine at his alma mater, the University of Florida. Some have suggested that Wayne Mixson should be recognized as the father of Florida agriculture.

Smelling the Roses—Reflections

During an interview, Wayne reflected about his life. "I am now ninety-four and Margie is in her late eighties. Both of us have remained active in civic and charitable organizations and events since I left public office. As I attempt to provide a meaningful, descriptive account of my life in this biography, I cannot avoid the realization that throughout my long life, my God and Creator has continually showered me with blessings.

"The first of these blessings was being born into a Christian, hard-working, and loving family, and then being raised in a rural farm environment. In combination, these benefits developed within me the values, ethics, and beliefs that have guided my actions throughout my life. Another blessing was the foundational education which was provided in the rural, South Alabama public school system which I attended. The work of those dedicated, capable teachers who nurtured and led me in those early days prepared me for the higher levels of education which were ahead.

"I was blessed to survive those terrible years of World War II while I served in the Navy's blimp program. I received another huge blessing when I was given the opportunity to attend schools such as Columbia in New York and Wharton at the University of Pennsylvania for undergraduate studies while in the Navy. The perspective this experience provided me in exposure to northern, urban culture and the prestige these fine schools added to my credentials were invaluable.

"Next came my greatest blessing, named Margie Grace. We have now been married sixty-nine wonderful years! What a blessing to be able to spend that many years in the company of a woman like her!! Throughout my life Margie has stood at my side, sharing every joy and pain as we worked as a team through every phase of our lives.

"I was blessed with the guidance and insight which led me to decide to return to farming instead of following a business career. The opportunities to buy land at the right time and to create a modern farm were more blessings. My significant involvement with the Farm Bureau organization provided me a deeper insight to Florida's agricultural community, the farming leadership, state government, and even federal government, which proved to be very important to my future.

"Then I was blessed with the good fortune to win my run for the legislature, and then to develop a strong backing in the North Florida region which enabled me to win the seat for six successive elections with little serious opposition. I was blessed with the unique opportunity to participate in the rewriting of the Florida constitution and the subsequent reorganization and streamlining of state government. I was also fortunate that during this era the Democratic Party still contained a large block of conservative voters and representatives. Otherwise, I would have been a conservative Republican and would not have been partnered with Bob Graham in his quest to become governor of Florida.

"I have always loved aviation. As a young man I earned certification as an aircraft mechanic. Then when I entered the Navy during the war, I earned the opportunity to fly in the Navy blimp program, and later in life my lifestyle enabled me to justify ownership of a private aircraft. I consider all of this involvement with aviation to have been a blessing.

"I found my career as a legislator, and later as the lieutenant governor, very fulfilling. I always felt I was accomplishing much needed progress in the areas of industrial development for Florida, creation of jobs for thousands of workers, helping the environment, improving the education system in our state, and aiding in the progress of Florida's agricultural industries. All of these were blessings.

"Margie and I were both blessed when Margie was cured of cancer. Otherwise, we have enjoyed good health throughout our long lives. We have been blessed with a loving, happy relationship.

As a result of all of my life's activities, I am blessed with a long list of great friends and supporters. All I can do is say, 'Thank you, Lord!'"

My Legacy

As Governor Bob Graham's final term approached its end in the early months of 1986, many expected Wayne Mixson to announce and launch a campaign to become Florida's next governor. He was well known and respected throughout the state, was acceptable to both philosophical elements of the Democratic Party, and was certainly in line for the position. Most insiders felt he would be victorious if he decided to seek the governorship.

Wayne discusses this critical career decision. "As the end of our second term approached and my closest friends and supporters began raising funds in an attempt to draft me into making the decision to run for governor, I was faced with the most difficult decision of my life. I realized that I did have a good chance of winning the prestigious position of governor of Florida.

"One important factor in my decision not to run for governor was the tremendous work we had already accomplished during my work as the lieutenant governor during the Graham administration. My strongest motivation had always been to convert Florida from having an antibusiness attitude into one of the leading states in industrial development and jobs creation. I wanted to bring those jobs to Florida in order to provide a better life for those thousands of farm families who were displaced as technology modernized the farming industries. If this task had remained undone, I would have run for governor. However, I felt we had already accomplished that goal.

"As I look back over my political career, I take great pride in some of the accomplishments we achieved during those years. Of course, as I have already stated, converting Florida into a national leader in industrial recruitment and development of international commerce is probably what I consider to be the greatest achievement.

"Another source of pride for me is the work we did in rewriting the Florida constitution and the subsequent reorganization of state government. The positive impacts of those changes were dramatic and are continuing today.

"Also, the creation of the $25,000 homestead exemption, the limits we established on property taxes, and the Greenbelt Laws which created a system of fair property tax assessment for farm properties were all improvements to Florida's taxation programs which I either sponsored or promoted. These approaches are still serving taxpayers in our state.

"And finally, the work accomplished during my many years as chairman of the Agricultural Commission has enhanced and protected Florida's agricultural industries, which continue to constitute a major portion of the state economy. I also take great satisfaction in having helped create the School of Veterinary Medicine at the University of Florida.

"My hope is that many years from now, long after I am gone, a Florida family will be driving down Highway 73 in Jackson County, and one of the children in the car will see the highway marker designating the road as the Wayne Mixson Highway, and will ask, 'Daddy, who was Wayne Mixson?' In response, the parent will say, 'Wayne Mixson was a farmer and politician from Jackson County who loved Florida, and his work helped us all.'"

Former Governor John Wayne Mixson died peacefully at his Tallahassee home on the morning of July 8, 2020, at the age of ninety-eight. Margie Grace was faithfully at his side, as she had been for the past seventy-two years.

The governor did get to see this finished biography before his death.

ADDENDUM

CHAPTER TWELVE

MEMORIES OF THE GRAHAM-CRACKER YEARS

An Interview with Former Governor Bob Graham and First Lady Adele Graham

Throughout Wayne Mixson's political career, his personal goals were the creation of new jobs in Florida through industrial development to replace the jobs lost from technological advances, and protecting agricultural interests in the face of massive population inflow and the resulting rapid development of land. For Bob Graham, his areas of primary concern were improving Florida's education systems and protecting Florida's delicate environment as the state's population multiplied and sprawling urbanization occurred. When these two great legislators came together, their administration's programs made great strides forward in all four of these important areas, during a critical time for the state.

Although this writing is the biography of Wayne Mixson, we felt that it would be appropriate to include a chapter from an interview with Bob and Adele Graham, since the eight years they occupied the executive branch of Florida's government represented the apex of Wayne's career. This interview was conducted by me, Sid Riley, on the University of Florida campus in Gainesville, Florida, at his office in the Graham Center on January 22, 2020. It was a chilly, blustery day as my daughter Allison and I parked and walked a few blocks across the well-groomed campus to our meeting.

As stated, throughout his years of public service as a Florida legislator, Florida governor, and U.S. senator, a primary objective for Bob Graham has been the enhancement of public and university education. Thus, it is only natural that upon his retirement from government in 2005, he entered the academic world. He immediately served two years as a senior research fellow at the Belfer Center for Science and International Affairs at Harvard University. While there he worked with the Harvard Kennedy School which conducts classes, seminars, and research into a variety of social issues, such as climate change, the impact of technology on society, and other issues of our time.

This experience at Harvard with the Kennedy program of studies prepared Bob Graham for his return to his home state, where he began the foundation of the Bob Graham Center for Public Service at the University of Florida. This new program, under the College of Liberal Arts and Sciences, is today housed in Pugh Hall, a new facility opened in 2010 to house the Graham Center. Its stated mission is to train the next generation of Florida leaders. It conducts courses and symposiums on social issues such as human rights, U.S.-Middle East Relations, Florida politics, climate change impact in Florida, immigration, and other timely topics.

I began the visit by giving the governor a draft copy of the manuscript of Wayne Mixson's biography, and demonstrating how the book was divided into Part I, which told of his life before he entered the Florida legislature in 1967, and Part II, which detailed his twenty years of public service as a legislator, lieutenant governor, and governor. We also reviewed the pictures that are in the book, especially those which included Governor Graham and his wife, Adele.

We were given a warm greeting, and soon we were in the former governor's office. In an earlier telephone conversation, I had asked the governor if he preferred to be addressed as "Governor" or "Senator." He responded that he actually preferred "Bob," but if it had to be more formal, he preferred Governor. "It certainly speaks well for a person's life accomplishments if he has the privilege of choosing from those options," I stated.

We began the interview with a discussion of his ancestry and family. Bob Graham's parents were Ernest R. "Cap" Graham and Hilda Simmons Graham. Ernest Graham moved to South Florida in 1921 to set up a sugar cane farming operation for Pennsylvania Sugar Company. Eventually the sugar company discontinued operations, and Graham was able to purchase 3,000 acres for his own farming and dairy operation. Located only sixteen miles from downtown Miami, and ten miles from the site of today's Miami International Airport, at the time he purchased the property it was still "out in the country."

The senior Graham became active in South Florida politics, serving as a Florida state senator from 1937 until 1944. He made a run for the governorship in 1944 but failed to win the Democratic nomination. From this legacy it was only natural that at least one of his children would become a legislator, and perhaps even run for the governorship.

Former governor Bob Graham's lifelong interest in Florida's environment, agriculture, and education system is genetic, since his father was a farmer, served on the Dade Drainage Commission, and was on the State Highway Board. Ernest was an early environmentalist, with a deep concern for protecting the ecology of the Everglades. He was also an early advocate for the creation of a state university in Dade County. Although it did not happen in his lifetime, today the Florida International University Student Union is named in his honor.

It is only natural that when legislators Bob Graham and Wayne Mixson joined to form the Graham-Cracker ticket and won the reins to the executive branch of Florida's government in 1978, they would have many common interests. They were both from farming families and had a deep love for the land and a concern for its protection, they both wanted to enhance and protect Florida's agricultural industries as rapid development occurred, and they worked to improve and expand Florida's education systems. In 2005 the Sunshine Skyway Bridge was renamed the Bob Graham Sunshine Skyway Bridge in his honor, since it was rebuilt during his administration, after the original bridge was severely damaged in a tragic accident.

After finishing his primary education at Miami Senior High School, Bob Graham earned his bachelor's degree at the University of Florida, and then his law degree from Harvard Law School in 1962. In 2006 the University of Florida College of Arts and Sciences awarded him a doctorate in the field of public service.

As Miami's continuing growth reached the boundaries of the Graham farm, they were tempted to take one of the offers being tendered by developers to sell the land. The family had previously bought land in South Georgia for a pecan and beef cattle operation, realizing that the Florida family farmland would eventually be developed.

"The family decided not to sell the land, and instead develop it ourselves, with my older brother, Bill, heading the company," he explained. Today the site of the old Graham dairy farm is the bustling town of Miami Lakes. It is an incorporated suburb of Greater Miami, with over 30,000 residents, 1,700 thriving businesses, 23 lakes, parks, schools, and a municipal government. Bob stated that the development of the properties is projected to last another fifteen years.

Bob Graham recalls first meeting Wayne Mixson when they both entered the Florida House of Representatives after the special election of 1967. "We met at a meeting and reception that was conducted for new legislators. Through our years of time in the Florida legislature, we shared participation in many official meetings and social events." Bob specifically remembers Wayne's assistance in obtaining the passage of the urban development bill. He recognized the fact that Wayne served as a moderating influence, often helping those holding opposing opinions to compromise on important legislation.

Bob also experienced the excitement that first term of taking part in the 1967-68 redrafting of the Florida constitution, and the reorganization of Florida's government. "I was especially proud of our accomplishments in education and reorganization of the executive branch, increasing the power of the governor," he said.

I asked him why he switched to the Florida Senate in the election of 1969. "I simply felt that I could be more effective in achieving my goals as a state senator," he replied. "I was especially interested in providing easier access to the universities, expanding the university system, providing statewide growth management, and developing the funding formula for K-12 schools."

Finally, the conversation moved to the governorship. It began with his process of choosing who would be his running mate, seeking the office of lieutenant governor. "Wayne was the front runner from the very start of the selection process. We were looking first for a man of unquestionable integrity, who had a positive following throughout the state. The fact that Wayne Mixson was a political leader from North Florida, with twelve years of legislative experience, and was well known and liked throughout the state, made him our first choice. He had just announced his intent to retire from politics, so I knew that my main job would be to change his mind," Bob explained.

"Shortly after I announced my intent to run, after conferring with my family and some close friends, we decided to ask Wayne to meet with us in Tampa to discuss the possibility of him joining our team. I especially wanted my brother Bill to be at the meeting with Wayne, since I respected his opinions. The meeting went very well. We discussed our areas of agreement and the few subjects where we were not totally in agreement, and finally developed an outline of what the primary objectives of our administration would be, and for what areas each of us would be responsible."

When Bob Graham and Wayne Mixson consummated that agreement, they forged a union between the liberal-leaning South Florida urban Democrats and the conservative-leaning North Florida rural Democrats. This combination created an administration that would be able to move important legislation into laws that would benefit the citizens of Florida for many generations to come.

"Within a few days I called Wayne and invited him to be my running mate for the job of lieutenant governor of Florida. He accepted, and we were off to the races."

After that initial selection meeting, they held several subsequent meetings regarding the campaign platform, how to handle answering questions on pertinent issues, and developing a strategic game plan for the campaign. "Of course I was involved in the '100 Workdays' project, where I pledged to spend 100 days working at 100 ordinary, blue-collar jobs across the state. Wayne and Margie borrowed a Winnebago motor home we owned, and they made a campaign tour around the state.

"It was during those workdays that I encountered one of the situations that unemployed, destitute people are sometimes faced with as they deal with the bureaucracy. I was applying for aid at a government office in Tampa, after spending the night in the YMCA shelter. While waiting for my turn I needed to use the restroom. I saw a sign on the door that said, 'Government Employees Only.' When I asked, the woman told me in a firm voice that I would have to go elsewhere. At that moment I resolved that if I won the election, removing that practice would be my first official act. Today the sign is on display in my Miami Lakes office.

"That idea was a great campaign activity. We got tremendous press attention, I learned a lot, and I met many wonderful people. That year of campaigning became a blur of rallies, dinners, events, speeches, and shaking thousands of hands. I think all of our team, Wayne, Margie, Adele, and myself, put all of our energies and skills into the effort. In looking back, it was a wonderful experience to visit with the people of the state, to energize our support, and create a strong bond within our group. Actually, it was fun . . . and we won."

Then Bob recalled the day they were inaugurated, which was also in January, forty years earlier. "It is cold outside today, but it was really, really cold on our inauguration day. In 1940 Allen Morris, a writer for the *Miami Herald* had said that it would be a 'cold day' when a South Florida Democrat was elected Governor of Florida . . . and appropriately, it snowed on my inauguration day!"

At this point I asked the governor what he felt were the most significant accomplishments of the Graham-Mixson administration. "Wayne and I always referred to the 'Three E's' as being what we focused on. These were Education, Environment, and Economy. Together, with support from the legislators of that time, we made some very significant advances in those fields."

He was correct. During their eight years in control of the executive branch of Florida's government, they were responsible for significantly expanding the state university system; instituting environmental programs such as the creation of water management districts throughout the state, each with a commission and permitting authority; initiating the Save the Manatee program and working to preserve the Everglades; and, under Wayne's direction, enhancing the State Department of Commerce, making Florida a more business-friendly state, moving the state from last place to first place in new jobs creation, and pushing open the floodgates of international trade, making Florida a major participant in global commerce.

Then I probed a more delicate area. "Governor, I know that there were a couple of incidents, such as the unitary tax, that could have caused conflict between you and Wayne. How did you approach those situations?"

"Well, there were a few things that came up where there was a distance between Wayne's opinion and mine, but we were always able to come to an agreement in common ground. We had a bond of mutual respect for each other's honesty and integrity that enabled us to handle these things. Plus, we were friends."

I next asked Governor Graham about his experiences as the U.S. senator from Florida in Washington. "What made you decide to run for the Senate?" I asked. "Well, I could not run for another term as governor due to Florida's term-limit law. I was not yet ready to retire, and I felt that I could continue working for the benefit of our state from the federal level," he responded.

I continued, "During your time in Washington, what do you consider the most important accomplishments?" He thought for a moment and then said, "When I had to resign the governorship a few days before the term expired, it moved Wayne into the governor's chair. I am glad that it worked out that way; he certainly deserves to have that honor bestowed upon him. As to accomplishments while I was in Washington, during my eighteen years as a U.S. senator I was able to continue initiatives that we had started in Florida while I was governor. I continued supporting education and environmental protection initiatives in Florida and throughout the nation.

"In 1990 I sponsored legislation for a joint federal-state program for the restoration of the Everglades. I served as the chairman of the Senate Intelligence Committee, and I was appointed co-chairman of the investigation commission after the 9/11 attacks."

I ended the interview with Bob Graham by asking him if he feels that Wayne could have won election if he had decided to run for governor. "Wayne Mixson was well liked and respected by almost everyone, he had the experience, and had statewide name recognition. He certainly had a very good chance of winning if he had wanted the job," he answered as we prepared to leave.

Our next interview was scheduled shortly after lunch with the former First Lady of Florida, Adele Graham. Bob called before we departed, alerting her that we were through at his office and would be there on time. He also gave us instructions on how to find their new residence.

A few months earlier, the Grahams had moved from their longtime family home in Miami Lakes to an upscale retirement center in Gainesville, Florida, so that Bob could continue his work full time at the Graham Center. As we arrived, Adele greeted us at the door, which featured several empty boxes . . . documentation that unpacking was still underway.

She invited us into their well-appointed home, which featured many memorabilia photographs of their travels and careers. Of course, the photos also featured the usual favorite family members and memorable events. Bob and Adele Graham had four daughters and currently enjoy eleven grandchildren.

We began by asking Adele about her family and how she met Bob. "My parents were Mildred Moore Khoury and Gabriel Robert Khoury. My father was an immigrant from Beirut, Lebanon, and my mother was from Ohio. They moved to Florida in 1920. I met Bob while we were students at the University of Florida. I went to the dean of students' office to discuss a problem I was having in a science class, and met Bob as I was leaving the building. During our conversation, he offered to tutor me in the class. We married when I was a junior and Bob was a senior.

"When he graduated from the University of Florida and decided to go to Harvard for his law degree, we moved to Boston. I finished college at Boston University and started teaching English and History at a middle school in Wellesley, Massachusetts, while he was finishing Harvard Law School. Then we moved to Miami Lakes.

"While he was a legislator, we would move to Tallahassee each time the legislature was in session, then back to Miami Lakes during the other months. Of course, in February of 1979 we moved into the governor's mansion."

"Did you know Margie before you began working together on Bob's campaign for governor?" I asked. "Yes, while Bob was a legislator, we both went to several events and various meetings and I recall meeting her then. Of course, we became much closer friends during that year of campaigning. We always enjoyed each other's company, and had good times. I remember going to London with them on the Concord. That was a great trip."

"Margie has told me that out of all of her travels with Wayne, she always enjoyed her trips to London the most. Adele, what place in the world would be your favorite?"

"I would have to say that I enjoy Beirut, Lebanon, the most, because of the personal relationship my family has with that country. I have extended family there on my father's side. I always enjoyed experiencing their lifestyle and culture although, like Margie, I enjoyed London, too."

Next, I asked Adele what areas she focused on while serving as the first lady of Florida. She thought for a moment, then replied "I tried to encourage school volunteerism and working with the elderly through a 'Community Cares' program. One thing that we started while living in the mansion was making the historic mansion more available for the public. There are a lot of important historical artifacts and pictures on display there, and I felt the public should be able to visit them. With Margie's participation we began a program of scheduled tours.

"Margie was instrumental in establishing a well-organized and educated group of docent volunteers to welcome visitors to the mansion. She was a good friend and helpmate during the nine years we were together. Happily, that accessibility policy has continued since we departed."

As I was driving back to Jackson County the next day, I thought about the Graham family and the interviews. I now have a deeper appreciation for the Graham dynasty and the tremendous impact that it has had on Florida, in the ninety-eight years since Cap Graham started his farm in Dade County in 1922.

TESTIMONIALS

Governor Bob and Mary Jane Martinez
Tampa, Florida

Governor Wayne Mixson is a Florida treasure, elected to the Florida House of Representatives in 1966 when the federal court mandated Florida to reapportion the legislature on a one man-one vote concept and hold a special election. He subsequently served our great state for twenty years as a state representative, lieutenant governor, and governor.

I first met Governor Mixson in 1967 when I was the Hillsborough Classroom Teachers Association's executive director and lobbyist and he was a member of the Florida House of Representatives. What struck me when I met with him was his thoughtfulness and the attention he gave to the subject matter. A true gentleman from Florida's Panhandle.

Governor Bob Graham made a very wise decision when he selected Wayne Mixson to be his lieutenant governor running mate. His knowledge of state government, Florida's Panhandle, and agriculture was a great asset in the 1978 election.

I developed a good relationship with Governor Mixson during my 1986 governor's transition period. When Governor Graham resigned three days early as governor of Florida to be sworn in as Florida's United States senator, Lt. Governor Mixson became Governor Mixson. My governor's transition team and I worked with him so he could fully enjoy the experience of being Florida's governor. He and First Lady Margie Grace Mixson did a wonderful job.

Florida is a better place because of Wayne and Margie Mixson's public service. Thank you for all you have done for the citizens of Florida.

Bob Martinez

Personal Thoughts

Governor Kenneth H. MacKay Jr.
Ocklawaha, Florida 32179

Wayne Mixson came into the legislature as a North Floridian at a time when the political power in Florida was shifting southward. At that time, the legislature met sixty days every other year "whether it needed to or not."

Wayne combined the political skills necessary to survive in North Florida with the necessary substantive skills and courage to help lead the effort to redirect the focus of Florida government toward the critical environmental and political needs of Central and South Florida. Wayne showed it was possible to be both conservative and also activist, when the circumstances required.

As a supporter of Bob Graham, I often worked closely with Wayne. He is a man of integrity.

Buddy MacKay

(Kenneth "Buddy" MacKay was the 42nd governor of Florida.)

For the Biography of John Wayne Mixson
by Senator Bill Nelson

Wayne Mixson has been a good friend since 1972; my goodness, that's been forty-seven years! When I first met him, he was already an accomplished legislator and leader in state government. Tinges of silver hair, a deep pleasant southern accent, and a razor-sharp mind on legislative tactics made him someone to look up to for a brand new young representative from central Florida.

Since my family had come to Florida in 1829 and settled in the adjacent county to Wayne's Jackson County, we immediately had a bond that grew into a lasting friendship, which included our wives, Margie and Grace.

A Southern gentleman, a successful farmer, an effective legislator, these are just some of the things that people say about him. But there is more. He is a good man who cares about his neighbors and loves his country. His heart is filled with love.

And that is why he was successful in whatever he did, in government and out. He treated folks with just plain courtesy and respect. He was also bipartisan and looked out for the state and country first. No excessive partisanship here.

He's remembered favorably by all who know him because he is a gentleman.

Clearly that reference in the Good Book applies to Wayne, "Well done thy good and faithful servant."

Bill Nelson
November 22, 2019

Governor Wayne Mixson—A Man Unlike Any Other
Personal Thoughts from Gregg A. Alexander, M.D.

Most of those who know Wayne Mixson have probably become acquainted with him through family, social, political, or business channels, or even from his rural background, his stint in the Navy, or from one of the schools he attended. I initially knew of him from newspaper accounts while he served his terms as Florida's lieutenant governor and briefly as governor, but those accounts did not give significant insight into the character of the man holding those offices. For me, in those days, Wayne Mixson was another politician. But all of that changed.

For nearly twenty-five years I have led a Sunday School class at Trinity United Methodist Church known as "Bible Journeys." Even that many years ago the seeds of theological and social liberalism were taking root in the United Methodist Church, and I often became a kind of fish swimming against the stream. Our class has been true to the Bible, and the messages I have presented have reflected the intent of the original Biblical authors in the original languages and in the contexts in which they were originally written. I have never tried to tell God "what He meant to say." I follow the Bible in the same way that a Supreme Court originalist follows the Constitution, and that makes me a conservative Christian. And it was into that setting that Wayne and Margie Mixson came one Sunday morning in 2001, and it wasn't because of me, but because of the earnest effort of that class to plumb the depths of Biblical Truth and apply to our lives what we learned. And the Mixsons knew they had found a home.

From that time forward I have seen Wayne occasionally in my office, periodically at his home, and faithfully—every Sunday—a few feet away in that classroom. And what he regularly offered and contributed put his larger-than-life personality and character in full view. He was philosopher, theologian, historian, poet, color commentator, and court jester. He knew the old hymns, the old poems, the classic books, and the political heavy hitters, and he knew when to draw and speak on that immense storehouse of knowledge, and when not to. He could often finish a Bible verse before I could read it to its conclusion. He was a joy always, and not only to me, but to everyone. He lit up the room, and he lightened the mood. His mind was always awake, and he enlightened the minds who took in his words.

At his home there would always be a stack of books by his favorite chair, and he could go through a book a day. But if you borrowed a book or a magazine from him, you might have a little trouble getting through it for there would always be the expected plethora of multicolored squiggled underlines giving a rough estimate as to how many times that item had been read by him.

Wayne and his ageless wife, Margie, are two of the most memorable people of my life. Although the places and the times and the situations of our lives have been limited, the impact of Wayne and Margie on my life has been long and large and widespread. For me, Wayne has truly been a man unlike any other.

Dr. Gregg Alexander
Tallahassee, Florida

Testimonial Statement from Amos H. Morris

Many years have passed since I first met Wayne Mixson, shortly after he moved to Jackson County from Alabama. (It is rumored that he was run out of Alabama for mishandling hogs . . . HA.)

My Alzheimer's is affecting me at times these days, but I can clearly remember the many occasions when Wayne Mixson came out to my farm for special events such as barbeques, fish fries, and the annual corn boils, as well as the times he just came by for a visit. Through those many years, I would have to say that Wayne has been one of my dearest friends. He has always been one of those people I could talk to about Jackson County, state government, or national issues. He always had an ear ready to listen.

On several occasions I was privileged to escort him around to review and evaluate the devastation after floods, storms, fires, and other disasters. I also fondly remember the times we fished and quail hunted together. He was one of the finest marksmen of quail that I ever saw. He used a sweet 16-gauge shotgun, and rarely missed.

On my eightieth birthday my friends and family arranged a large party for me. I was especially honored, and touched, when Wayne came and served as master of ceremonies for the evening. Not many people are privileged to have a former governor as the MC at their birthday celebrations.

In my opinion, as an elected official representing Jackson County, he has been one of the finest and most honest politicians in Florida. He eagerly assisted me when I promoted the passage of legislation to stop the importation of exotic game and snakes into Florida from foreign countries. We failed in our effort back then, and today the python snakes are costing the state millions as they try to eradicate the growing nuisance. Wayne and I made little headway, but we can say we tried. The opposition to the legislation claimed that it would take too much money out of the economy, since it was a significant business in Florida.

I would state that Wayne has always been one of the best stewards of Florida's land, water, and other resources. Many of the programs he helped make into laws are still protecting our resources today.

I could easily go on and on and on about the good he has done for the state, for agriculture, and for Florida's economy. I wish we had more politicians like Wayne Mixson.

My door will always be open to him and Margie.

Amos Morris

Note: Amos Morris is a well-known Jackson County farmer, businessman, and outdoorsman. He is especially renowned for his culinary skills and is regularly called upon to cook or cater for special functions, some as far away as Atlanta. Amos has always been a highly respected Jackson County citizen. He has known Wayne Mixson for over fifty years.

ABOUT THE AUTHOR
SIDNEY W. RILEY

Sid Riley was raised in a rural setting in northwestern Kentucky in the Ohio River delta near the town of Morganfield. After graduating from Morganfield High School in 1957, he earned his Bachelor of Science degree from Georgia Institute of Technology in Atlanta, Georgia. While in college he enrolled in the Air Force ROTC and earned his commission as a United States Air Force officer upon graduation. He served one tour of duty, assigned to Strategic Air Command as leader of a management engineering team.

He was married to Judy Mathews-Riley in 1960. They have a son and a daughter, six grandchildren, and five great-grandchildren. They have now been married sixty-two years.

He separated from the military in 1965 and began employment with an Atlanta-based consulting engineering firm. As the organization expanded over the next five years, Sid became a vice president and director of the forty-man consulting group. He engaged in extensive travel, domestically and internationally, as he sold, supervised, and conducted engineering projects in hundreds of client-owned manufacturing plants. He wrote many technical articles which were widely published in trade journals during this era.

In 1970 he sold his home, put together a financial package, and moved to Marianna, Florida, to start an apparel manufacturing plant with one hundred employees in nearby Sneads, Florida. Since this plant was located in Wayne Mixson's congressional district, he soon became acquainted with the young state representative. A few years later, Riley acquired a larger, three hundred-employee plant in Marianna, Florida.

In 1979 he sold the plants to a larger company and partnered with a college roommate to form Jones-Riley & Associates, an engineering consulting company. Over the ensuing twenty-five years, he traveled and worked throughout the United States, Canada, Mexico, Puerto Rico, the Caribbean, Central America, and South America, performing engineering and management consulting services for hundreds of companies. Since he was a pilot, Sid purchased a small airplane and accomplished much of this travel in that manner, accumulating over 12,000 flight hours. During this period, he was regularly published in trade journals. He also published a technical book about a particular manufacturing process.

As manufacturing began to slow down in America, Sid was approaching retirement age. In 2005 he had begun writing a popular political column, "Getting It Right by Sid Riley," in the local newspaper, the *Jackson County Times*. Eventually he became managing editor and part owner of the paper. During the next eight years, under his management and participation, the paper became widely read throughout Jackson County. During this period, Sid maintained a personal relationship with Wayne Mixson.

Due to a serious illness, Sid sold his interest in the paper in 2013, and was unable to work for the next four years. As he reached full recovery, a mutual friend, Bill Stanton, encouraged Wayne Mixson to solicit Sid for the task of writing a biography of the former governor and legislator. The project began in 2016 and was completed in 2021.